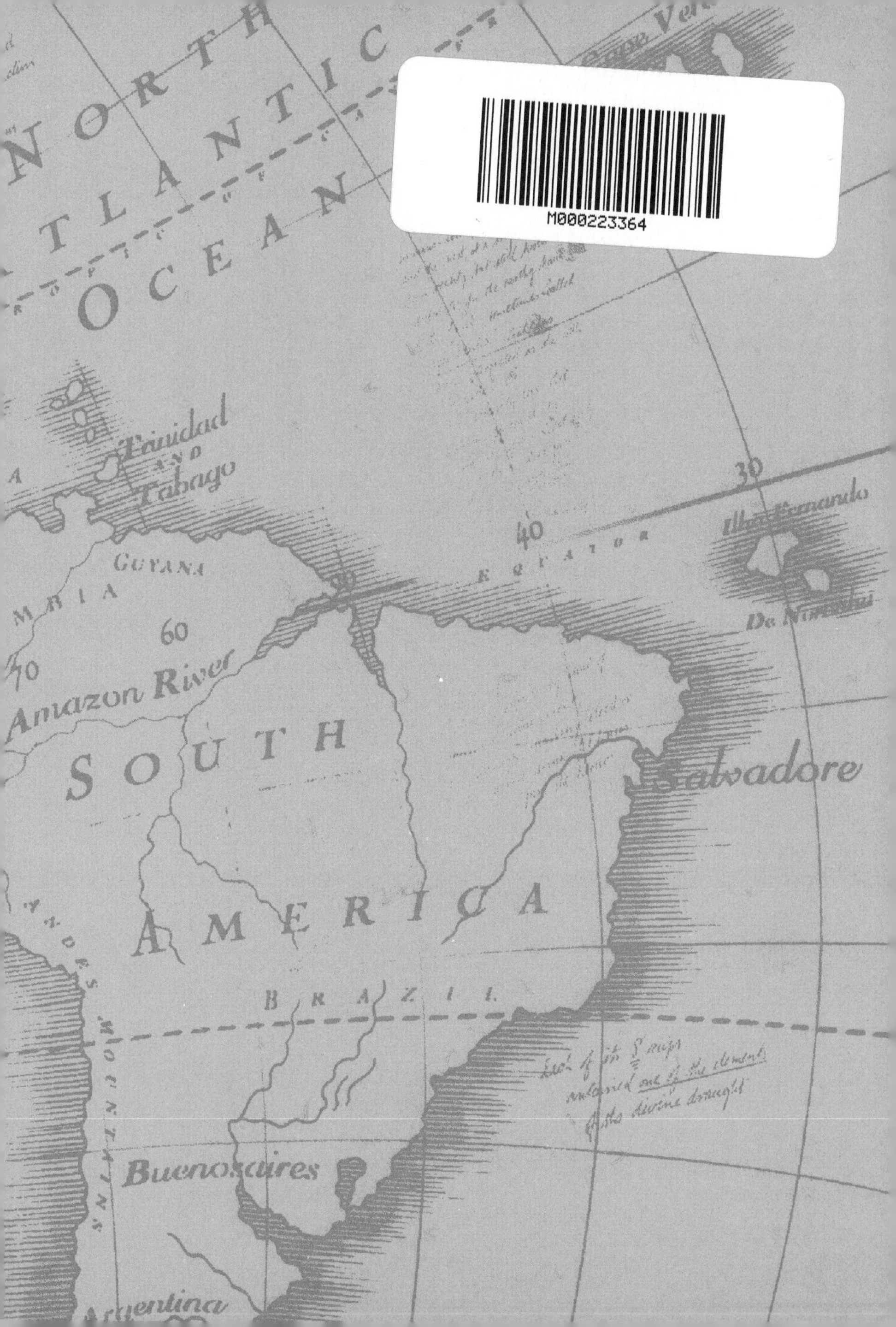

NORTH

ATLANTIC

OCEAN

Cape Verde

Trinidad AND Tobago

GUYANA

COLOMBIA

Amazon River

ANDES MOUNTAINS

SOUTH

AMERICA

BRAZIL

Buenos aires

Argentina

Salvadore

Ilha Fernando

De Noronha

EQUATOR

30

40

60

70

20

THE

INDIANA JONES™

HANDBOOK

THE

INDIANA JONES™

HANDBOOK

THE COMPLETE ADVENTURER'S GUIDE

BY DENISE KIERNAN AND JOSEPH D'AGNESE

QUIRK BOOKS
PHILADELPHIA

Library of Congress Cataloging in Publication Number: 2007937901

ISBN 978-1-59474-221-7

Printed in Singapore

Typeset in Bembo, Bodoni, Bulldog, and Candida

Designed by Doogie Horner
Illustrations by Roger Petersen

Distributed in North America by Chronicle Books
680 Second Street
San Francisco, CA   94107

10 9 8 7 6 5 4 3 2 1

Quirk Books
215 Church Street
Philadelphia, PA   19106
www.quirkbooks.com

www.indianajones.com

CONTENTS

WALTER DONOVAN
As you can now see, Dr. Jones, we are on the
verge of completing a quest that began almost
two thousand years ago. We're just one step away.

INDIANA JONES
That's usually when the ground falls out from
underneath your feet.

INTRODUCTION

If you have taken it upon yourself to buy this book, you're probably not seeking the life of a traditional archaeologist, locked away in an ivory tower as you grade exams and jockey for tenure. Tedium may be a necessary part of your day-to-day existence, but you undoubtedly want more—travel, adventure, mystery. In short, you want a career not unlike that of Dr. Henry "Indiana" Jones Jr., the greatest archaeologist of all time. Well, you can have it. But you should know what you're getting yourself into.

As Dr. Jones once said, "Archaeology is the search for fact, not truth." If it's truth you're interested in, consider a career in philosophy. There are precious few indisputable truths in the life of an archaeologist. You will rarely follow maps that lead you to the precise location of a buried treasure. Seventy percent of all archaeology is done in a library, researching, reading, and accumulating data. You must use these facts to form your own conclusions.

That said, you may sometimes find yourself confronted with mysteries that your books haven't covered, so one cannot afford to ignore folklore and myth, which often describe real-life events in the form of a dramatic narrative. Remember that fact can get a little fuzzy out in the field. You will come across people and places that will turn all your ideas about fact on their heads. No book can fully prepare you for what you will encounter once you've left the confines of your campus, but this one provides a good start.

Drawing on the many adventures of the world's most famous archaeologist, *The Indiana Jones Handbook* will advise you on everything from basic planning and transportation tips to people skills, excavation techniques, and strategies for dealing with supernatural elements. Whenever possible, we've tried to mention how Dr. Jones and his companions have responded to similar situations.

Study these instructions, carry them with you in your rucksack, and most importantly, be sure to expect the unexpected. When you encounter elements that are not covered in these pages, you will—just like Indiana Jones—have to make it up as you go along. Good luck!

CHAPTER 1

EXPEDITION ESSENTIALS

A successful expedition depends on many things—some well within your control and others far beyond it. While there's not much you can do to prepare for, say, the Wrath of God, you can make sure you know the local customs, you've anticipated weather conditions, and you've brought along plenty of toilet paper.

There is no substitute for comprehensive planning. You will need food and shelter. You will need transportation. You will need first aid. And so will everyone on your team, which may feature more than a hundred people. This chapter will assist you in planning the basics of your expedition, but there is no way to anticipate everything you will encounter. At the end of the day—and it will likely be a very long day—your ability to improvise will be your greatest asset.

HOW TO PLAN AN EXPEDITION

Before you set out to recover the unrecoverable, get your facts in order. You may not have time to learn an obscure language such as Hovitos, but you can at least hire a guide who is fluent. And even if you think you're the world expert on a particular relic, be diligent and make sure that you know what you're getting yourself into. Here are some tips to keep in mind before you head out on what will likely be an unexpected and unknown adventure.

1. HAVE REASONABLE GOALS.

This guideline is a tough one for most successful archaeologists, who never could have achieved such remarkable feats without a ridiculous amount of optimism. But the truth is, you may not always find what you seek and, even if you do, you may not be able to take it with you or keep it once you return. Some items may slip in and out of your grasp for years. Dr. Indiana Jones knows this fact better than most, having spent much of his life striving to obtain—and keep—the Cross of Coronado. He also lost the prized Chachapoyan fertility idol to Rene Belloq. In short, no matter how hard you try, you will never have complete control over everything that is going to happen.

2. HIT THE BOOKS.

The more you can research in advance, the better prepared you'll be in the field. You must leave no stone—or yellowed, aging piece of parchment—unturned. Use all sources, including those of your rivals. There is always more information to be found, whether it comes from a library or from the mouth of a village elder. There are career archaeologists who have spent their entire lives studying just one particular artifact. Dr. Henry Jones, Sr., is one such scholar. His lifelong devotion to the study of Holy Grail lore was proved invaluable when he and Indy were finally face-to-face with the object of his lifelong obsession.

3. SECURE ADEQUATE FUNDING.

Expeditions can get pricey very quickly. You are undoubtedly aware that archaeology ranks right up there with philosophy as one of the worst ways to make a quick buck. Your teaching income probably does not leave extra money to dedicate to far-flung expeditions; that's where government and foundation grants, private funding, individual collectors, and museums come into play. But make sure you know who you're getting into bed with, so to speak. While the lure of hefty financial support can be dizzying, there is always a price. The financiers will demand control of the precious object you seek, and you may not like what they want to do with it. Indiana Jones has always preferred working with museums for this reason. Though he has also worked on expeditions funded by the government and individual collectors, those experiences were far from satisfactory. Consider Lao Che, the Shanghai crime lord who promised Indy a diamond if he would locate the remains of Nurhachi, the first emperor of the Manchu Dynasty—only to later double-cross Indy by poisoning him. With an academic grant, you will rarely face this kind of peril.

4. KNOW WHO YOU'RE WORKING WITH.

Assembling a good team is hard work. Unless you have time for a background check on everyone you deal with—and you won't—there is no way to completely trust your colleagues. All you can do is take precautions and do your best to ascertain everyone's motives as early as possible. Indiana Jones has learned the hard way that well-meaning collectors with deep pockets may have ulterior motives that conflict with your own, and that could get you tied up in a castle on the Austrian-German border. The smart, sassy blonde with all the right credentials might be impossible to resist. But resist her, if you can.

Remember that those who have signed on to work with you may, in fact, turn on you at any moment. It is a rare individual indeed who can resist the temptations that extraordinary treasures present. Of course, you may find yourself with expedition companions by default, rather than by your own choosing. Satipo and Barranca, the two interpreters who guided Indy into a Peruvian forest, were quick to betray him for their own selfish ends. Satipo tried to swipe the golden idol from Indy and abandoned him in a booby-trapped cavern without his trusty bullwhip. However, fate dealt harshly with both of those unsavory characters.

5. KNOW WHO YOU'RE WORKING AGAINST.

Keep your friends close, and your enemies closer. This statement is as true for archaeologists as it is for any ruthless businessperson or member of the underworld. The more time passes, the fewer bona fide "unknown" treasures are out there. If you are going after an artifact, chances are someone else is, too—or they already have it. Anticipate your rivals and learn as much about them as possible. And, as distasteful as it may seem, consider befriending them.

6. CONSIDER ALL SOURCES.

It's likely that none of the top archaeological journals mention anything about long-standing curses or deadly booby traps surrounding the prize you hope to obtain. But perhaps the local guides have shared rumors, folklore, and mystical tales about the treasure. Do you ignore them because they are not scholars? No, you do not. You thank them kindly for their information and remember that books do not have all the answers.

TOP TEN FINDS OF THE TWENTIETH CENTURY

1. ARK OF THE COVENANT (1936)

Discovered by Dr. Jones in the lost city of Tanis, Egypt, the Ark contains the actual stone tablets carried by Moses down from Mount Horeb. The Ark, a source of unspeakable power, is believed to be in a U.S. government repository, crate number 9906753, possibly in a secret desert base.

2. HOLY GRAIL (1938)

Though recovered by Indy in a temple built within the Canyon of the

Crescent Moon outside Iskenderun (formerly Alexandretta), the Grail was presumed lost in a temblor that rocked the temple. Prior to being lost, the Grail performed at least one unexplained "miracle"— saving the life of Henry Jones Sr.

3. SANKARA STONES (1935)

The stones are sacred symbols, or lingas, which were stolen by practitioners of a reborn Thuggee cult from various religious sites throughout India. Only five stones are believed to still exist. One stone was returned by Indy to the village of Mayapore, its rightful place. The whereabouts of the remaining four stones are unknown, but two were last seen during a hand-to-hand battle between Indy and a villainous thug, Mola Ram, as they fell to a river below.

4. CHACHAPOYAN IDOL (1936)

This golden fertility idol is a relic of the Chachapoyan warriors that scholars believe to be hidden in a booby-trapped cavern in Peru. Indy discovered the idol, but it was taken from him by the mercenary French archaeologist Rene Belloq. Belloq mysteriously disappeared in 1936, a presumed victim of the Wrath of God. The idol was not found among his personal effects, and is presumed lost to both the modern world and the Hovitos.

5. CROSS OF CORONADO (1938)

Originally discovered by looters in 1912, this fabled relic—a gift from

Cortes to Coronado in 1520—fell into the hands of a private collector and was finally recovered by Indy off the coast of Portugal.

---

6. KING TUT'S TOMB (1922)

The grave of Tutankhamen, an Egyptian pharaoh who died at age 19, is the best-preserved tomb of its kind to have survived to modern times. The boy ruler's reign is not especially notable, but because of the rich artifacts found in his famous tomb, he is today arguably the world's best-known ancient ruler.

---

7. THE NAZCA LINES (1927)

These fascinating geoglyphs—etched into the desert floor of Peru—form huge designs that can only be correctly interpreted from the air. A mystery to this day, they are believed by some to be devices used by ancient peoples to communicate with alien visitors.

---

8. DEAD SEA SCROLLS (1947)

These 850 papyrus documents, still in an excellent state of preservation, were discovered in caves around the Dead Sea. Among the writings are the earliest known copies of biblical texts.

---

9. CRYSTAL SKULLS (EARLY 20TH CENTURY)

These famous skulls—carved entirely from quartz stone—were discovered in Central America and are reputed to have supernatural powers. They may have been left on earth by alien beings. According to believers, about a dozen crystal skulls exist, though only five have been found.

---

10. MACHU PICCHU (1911)

The famous Lost City of the Incas was built on a Peruvian mountain-top at least forty years before Columbus's arrival in the New World. Unlike other cities conquered and destroyed by the Spaniards, Machu Picchu was abandoned by its original inhabitants.

HOW TO PACK FOR AN EXPEDITION

This can be tricky. You'll need to pack both survival necessities and research materials—and with all of those heavy reference books, you won't have the space to carry everything you like. So be prepared to rinse out your clothes several times. If you can keep a fair amount of luggage at your base of operations, that's great. Keep in mind that you cannot carry excess items while in the field. They will get in the way of your work and make it particularly difficult to escape if you find yourself being pursued in 100-plus degree heat by scimitar-wielding hired assassins.

CLOTHING

It has been said that you are what you wear, but on an expedition you should be more concerned with your well-being and the security of the artifacts than with your appearance. Here are some basic guidelines:

- **On your feet** Sturdy shoes or, ideally, boots that cover your ankle are a must. It's best if they are water resistant and have good support. Also pack socks—lots of them. You should always keep your feet dry. If you are going to bring extras of anything, make it socks, and wash them often.

- **On your body** Shirts and pants should be sturdy and made of cotton, twill, or anything that will breathe under hot conditions. Both should be long-sleeved to protect your skin from sun, insects, and scrapes. Pockets are always a good idea. Khaki or safari wear has always been a popular choice for Indy. You may wish to pack some items made of polypropylene if you are anticipating cold temperatures. Don't forget a good sturdy belt, since that will have to hold up not only your pants but your pistol and bullwhip as well.

  A durable and versatile jacket is also indispensable, both for chilly nights and for providing an extra layer of protection during the occasional dragging behind a truck. The leather bomber jacket is a classic and suitable choice.

- **On your head** A good hat is essential, especially to keep sun and wind from your eyes. The fedora has been the hat preferred by Dr. Jones since he was boy. After unsuccessfully challenging a band of looters who were stealing the Cross of Coronado, his consolation prize was the fedora worn by their rapscallion leader. It was hardly a substitute for a priceless relic that belongs in a museum, but apparently he liked the look. Admirers of Indiana's hat can find a similar style in

London at the Herbert Johnson Hat Shop. Try the "Australian" or "Poet" model, fitted with a Petersham ribbon.

A bandana is another handy item to have in your kit. In addition to wiping away sweat and protecting your head, a clean bandana can be used for everything from tying off wounds to filtering coffee.

- **Formal wear** You never know when you might be required to don a snazzy tux in order to complete a business transaction in an upscale nightclub. You always want to blend in, and having at least one nice garment to wear helps you cover your bases.

GEAR

You will need a sturdy bag to keep on your person, especially for those times when you are on foot and must travel light. We recommend a satchel instead of a backpack, but everyone has an individual preference. Indiana Jones is partial to a bag that was a precursor to the World War II MKVII gas mask bag.

The bag should contain the following:

- **Maps, diaries, and any relevant notes.** These will certainly aid your expedition—but remember that others may attempt to kill you for them. For this reason, be careful what you carry. Commit to memory as much sensitive material as possible and consider mailing your valuable papers to someone you trust, rather than keeping them with you.
- **First-aid kit.** This should include smelling salts, ace bandage, aspirin, epinephrine injections, instant cold compress, sterile gauze, and latex gloves, which are also excellent for handling fragile artifacts.

- **Adequate food and drinking water** per person for the duration of your trip.
- **Handheld PDA and cell phone** with GPS capabilities, including extra batteries, a charger, and a universal adapter.
- **Fisher Space Pen.** Ideal for writing under a variety of conditions, including upside-down.
- **Digital camera.** If your sketching abilities are less than admirable and you have adequate light, it is always advisable to keep a visual record of your dig. No flash, please.
- **Papers, crayons, and chalk for rubbings.** Sure, a digital camera can capture the basic image of any stone tablet. But if you want to record all the detailed nuances (and not worry about batteries running out), there is no substitute for a good rubbing.
- **Magnetic compass**
- **Waterproof matches and/or lighter**
- **Mini-flashlight**
- **Small mirror** with extendable shaft. Excellent for looking around corners in tight spaces such as tombs.
- **Swiss army knife.** No self-respecting archaeologist should leave home without one.
- **Resealable plastic bags.** These are ideal for protecting items from the elements, especially water. Always keep a few on hand.

1. BULLWHIP
2. CAMERA
3. CELL PHONE
4. MAPS
5. FIRST-AID KIT
6. POCKET KNIFE
7. JOURNAL
8. WATERPROOF MATCHES
9. DRINKING WATER
10. MINI-FLASHLIGHT
11. SMALL MIRROR

INDY ESSENTIALS

Back in the early days of archaeological expeditions, if you found yourself entombed in the desert you couldn't just whip out a cell phone and call for help. Here are the additional items that Indiana Jones is never without. You may wish to add them to your rucksack:

Bullwhip

Useful in a variety of situations (see "How to Use Your Bullwhip," page 24), the bullwhip does not take up a lot of room and can even be worn on your belt. Indiana Jones has had his since a close call with a lion in his youth, but you can get them from suppliers in the United States.

Firearms

Indy is partial to handy revolvers, including the Smith & Wesson hand ejector, the British Webley & Scott Mk. VI revolver, and the Colt New Service M1917 revolver. He has also on occasion needed a Browning HP P-35 semiautomatic pistol. But his adventures are hardly common. Most archaeologists have never given anyone a dirty look, let alone shot at them. Don't waste your shekels on a gun unless you have good reason to believe you need one.

HOW TO USE YOUR BULLWHIP

There are a lot of things that are associated with archaeology—bones, tombs, tiny little brushes—but perhaps no item is associated with Indiana Jones as much as his bullwhip. Dr. Jones perfected his "whipcraft" over many years of training and started his study when he was still a boy. He has long relied on it during his travels, and he thought it important to include information about bullwhips in this guide for the next generation of adventure-seeking archaeologists.

We may live in an age of high-tech weaponry, but the simple elegance of a bullwhip often proves useful in diverse, and often unfriendly, situations. Not only can it be used in conflicts with man or beast, but it is also handy for swinging over chasms, disarming adversaries, and lassoing loved ones. Other benefits of carrying a bullwhip are that it is easily packed, you can wear it, and it is easy to keep concealed. It is also one of the few weapons that will not set off any pesky airport alarms or draw undue attention from the X-ray machines.

It will take some time to perfect your bullwhip skills, so it's important to be patient. Here are some basic pointers to keep in mind.

If you like fly-fishing, you'll love cracking a whip. Some beginners find it useful to imagine they are casting a fishing line. Remember your follow-through.

Be aware of your surroundings. The reach of your whip plus the length of your arm can mean trouble for anyone within twelve or thirteen feet in all directions. Try to keep it away from anyone you don't intend to harm. Remember, it's all fun and games until someone scratches a cornea.

Also remember that the whip can fling dirt and debris far and fast— roughly 700 miles (or 1,125 km) per hour, in fact—so keep that in mind before demonstrating your skills at a family picnic.

Be aware of your own person, too. That means you might want to start your training wearing some protective gear, at least for your eyes. Otherwise, always watch your eyes and lips. Dr. Jones has the scar to show what happens if you don't.

OVERHEAD CRACK

This is the most dramatic maneuver at your disposal, and it's quite effective at keeping people—especially those who want to kill you—at a distance. The overhead crack visually announces your intention to get down to business.

- Seat the ball of the whip handle in your palm.
- Swing the whip in a circular fashion over your head. If you are right-handed, the natural way to do this is counter-clockwise.
- When you're ready to crack, pay attention to the position of the "cracker" or "popper"—the part of the whip at the very end that helps make the popping noise. When it is behind your head to the right, extend your arm forward.
- As you bring the whip forward, snap your wrist. This action causes the loop or arc formed in the length of the whip to shoot toward the cracker, which travels faster than the speed of sound and emits a cracking sound that is, in fact, a tiny sonic boom.

OVERHEAD CRACK

BEGIN WITH WHIP DOWN AT YOUR SIDE.

RAISE WHIP OVERHEAD IN A CIRCULAR MOTION.

BRING WHIP FORWARD AND SNAP YOUR WRIST.

FORWARD CRACK

This crack is good for targeting—and you may likely have some very unsavory targets to aim at in your travels.

- Raise your arm quickly but smoothly. Be aware of where your whip lies before doing so. You don't want it wrapping around your leg or foot—or someone else's—on the way up.
- Stop when your arm and hand are above your head. Your elbow should be aimed at your unlucky target.
- Your cracker will start to drop behind you. As soon as it does, most people step forward with their left leg (assuming they're right-handed). Others don't step at all. It's up to you.
- As you step, cast the whip forward as you would your trusty fishing rod. Your arm should be extended directly in front of you and pointed at your target, not down toward the ground.
- Snap your wrist.

WHIP IT UP

Other handy uses for the whip include its ability to wrap around an object or a person—be it a comely lounge singer or a fire poker in the hands of a ruthless, sadistic stooge. This technique is rather difficult and should be attempted only after you've perfected the two maneuvers described above.

The key to performing this skill is to "crack" the whip off to the side of the target. Once the cracker has cracked, the momentum will continue to carry the length of the whip through the air. Physics will do its job, and the whip will easily wrap around the waist of your target, who can then be pulled toward you and either kissed or concussed. Or both.

FORWARD CRACK

RAISE THE WHIP UNTIL IT'S ABOVE YOUR HEAD.

THE CRACKER WILL BEGIN TO DROP BEHIND YOU.

STEP FORWARD AND EXTEND YOUR ARM. SNAP YOUR WRIST.

This technique can be used to wrap the whip around a tree or other stationary object for swinging purposes. Remember that when you wrap the whip around, say, a tree limb overhead, you should swing so that the extended portion of the whip crosses on top of the part of the whip that is wrapped around the limb. That will help keep the whip from unwrapping too quickly.

Give a sharp tug on your whip; the tip will drop free, and the remaining coils will loosen. Give a few more gentle tugs, and the coils should work free. Once you've mastered your ability to wrap the whip around people and stationary objects, you can develop your skills even further and use your whip to disarm adversaries.

WARNING: When jumping over a chasm, it's foolish to let your partner go first—especially if you don't know him very well and he happens to be holding the priceless idol you just obtained.

HOW TO SURVIVE IF YOU ARE POISONED

There are so many ways for a ruffian to get out of paying an honest researcher for the work he was hired to do. The scoundrel can claim bankruptcy, try to pass a check he know won't clear, or, just to liven things up a bit, he may try to poison the stalwart archaeologist's cocktail.

Poison comes in many shapes and forms, from paint chips laced with lead to common garden flowers like foxglove. Because of this, there is no single cure for what ails you, but there are some strategies for both preventing poisoning and handling the situation if you do end up imbibing something deadly.

1. WATCH YOUR DIET.

When in the presence of armed individuals with a questionable respect for life, you should always practice defensive dining. It's never a good idea to eat or drink with your enemies, unless it would be insulting or suspicious not to do so (see "How to Blend In," page 72). Be even more vigilant if you and your host happen to be arguing over money. For these reasons, eating and drinking anything that is put in front of you without hesitation can be risky.

2. WATCH YOUR GLASS.

If you can, keep an eye on your food and drink at all times. In fact, if possible, watch your drink as it is being mixed. If you are at all suspicious of what has been handed to you, it is always better to err on the side of self-preservation. An easy way to rid yourself of a terrible tonic is to "accidentally" knock over your glass. Then politely excuse yourself to go to the bar to fetch a fresh—and ideally tamper-free—drink.

3. INSIST THAT YOUR HOST TASTE YOUR DRINK FIRST.

If you would like to throw your hosts for a loop, insist that they sip your drink or eat your food first. Blame it on an obscure custom from your very small, out-of-the-way neck of the woods in the United States. "It's an important tradition in my region to share the same glass with honored guests. Please—

CHOOSE YOUR DRINKING BUDDIES VERY CAREFULLY.

you drink and then I will do the same." For the sake of respecting another's customs, they should be happy to comply. However, if they refuse, you may wish to think twice before drinking up or digging in.

4. ASCERTAIN THAT YOU HAVE, IN FACT, BEEN POISONED.

You may or may not feel any immediate symptoms when you are first poisoned, so pay particular attention to subtle hints that may indicate you have been on the receiving end of a deadly libation. For example, if everyone seated at the table starts laughing after you've just taken a sip of your drink, that is a pretty big clue that you have been played. Seek immediate medical attention or start bartering for the antidote.

5. DON'T WAIT AROUND.

Just because there may be no immediate symptoms does not mean that they won't kick in at any moment. If you feel fairly certain that you have been poisoned—and if you have crossed a major player in the Shanghai underworld, it's quite likely—just assume that your suspicions are correct and take the appropriate measures.

6. DON'T ADD TO THE MIX.

Contrary to popular belief, it is not a good idea to try to neutralize the poison or induce vomiting by consuming mustard, vinegar, or saltwater. It tastes bad, and if you're on the road or in a night club you will probably not have time to go fishing through someone's kitchen.

7. GET THE ANTIDOTE.

The ideal way to treat yourself if you have ingested an otherwise unknown, exotic poison is to get your hands on the antidote. Indiana was poisoned by Lao Che, a disreputable gangster with a penchant for cremated remains. Getting the antidote from someone who revels in watching others suffer may be easier than you think. Anyone who has gone out of his way not only to poison you but to tell you about it likes to play head games. After they have enjoyed taunting you with the information that they've just poisoned you, they will want to continue their fun and move on to teasing you about the fact that they just so happen to have the antidote on them. It's just not as entertaining for sadistic thugs to poison you and then let nature take its course. They want to relish the experience. That can work to your advantage. As long as they have it, all you have to do is pry it from their devious little mitts. That may involve creating a distraction, physically threatening them, or bargaining—no matter how much hard-earned fortune it may cost you.

CHAPTER 2

GETTING AROUND
AND GETTING AWAY

The well-traveled archaeologist must be proficient in many modes of transportation. You can be sure that the moment you're in need of a sleek and speedy car or a hefty truck, you'll find yourself riding in a motorcycle side-car or on a camel. It goes without saying that you can expect gap-toothed, gun-wielding looters and scoundrels to be in pursuit—especially if you've just relieved them of a priceless antiquity. Here are some helpful hints about how to evade, escape, and survive while on the go.

HOW TO RUN ON TOP OF A MOVING TRAIN

No matter how hard you try, sooner or later you are going to have to take on a villain and his goons atop a moving train. The best advice we can offer is: Don't. Trains are lot tougher to handle today than they were in Indy's day. Even when traveling slowly, a modern freight train rolls about 50 to 60 miles per hour, compared to 15 or 25 miles per hour in those halcyon days of Utah in 1912. Granted, sometimes you don't have a choice. If the bad guys are hot on your tail, by all means scurry up a boxcar and man your ground. Just be smart about it.

1. APPROACH THE TRAIN ON HORSEBACK.

Ride your faithful steed alongside the moving train. Keep an eye out for ladders or steps. When these are in sight, spur the horse to speed up and keep pace with the moving train. Grab hold of the boxcar's ladder, unhook your feet from the stirrups, and goad the horse to ride ahead. His body will slip gently between your legs. Flex your arm muscles and pull yourself up so your legs don't drop to the tracks below. Find some decent footing and start climbing. The rungs of the ladder will go to the top of the boxcar. Keep climbing until you reach horizontal ground.

2. STAY LOW.

Even to passengers tucked safely inside the club car, trains feel a lot like dinghies on the open sea. They rock. They roll. They sway, fishtail, and shimmy. Your chances of getting through this ordeal are better if you keep your center of gravity low. Keep your head down, bend your knees, and crouch as you walk briskly across the top of the train. Watch your footing. Some boxcars have pronounced seams across the tops where the sheet metal is welded together; you don't want to trip on them. Others may have skylights or other openings that could spell disaster.

3. DON'T GO WITH THE FLOW.

As soon as you can, note the direction in which the train is traveling—then run in the opposite direction. This sounds counter-intuitive, but it makes perfect sense; as you jump the gaps between boxcars, the train will be moving forward under you, requiring you to jump a shorter distance. If you run with the train, you will always be forced to jump harder and faster to get over the gaps.

4. BE ALERT.

You'd think there would be nothing between you and the sky so high off the ground, but nothing is further from the truth. There are entirely too many things that could go wrong on top of a moving train. As a train takes a turn, its boxcars tilt. When that happens, hug the boxcar roof or you could be thrown onto the tracks or between the cars. Avoid climbing between cars during this time. The gap between two cars narrows on one side as they take a turn. Get between them and you'll be squashed like a bug. Keep an

eye out for power lines, low-slung lampposts, signage, mail-delivery plat-
forms, tunnel entrances, and angry rhinoceroses. Watch out for everything.
Everything, you hear?

5. KNOW YOUR GOAL.

We all agree this is not the optimum way to travel. You're there to do a job,
so get it done and get out of there. If you are trying to gain entrance to a
specific car, pinpoint it in the distance and work your way toward it
deliberately. If you must engage in fisticuffs with another party, be brisk
about it. Bend your knees, use short, focused blows, and dispatch the thug
mercilessly. Work the face, solar plexus, and gut. No high-flying round-
house punches. Keep in mind: Your foe will be desperate. As we have tried
to make clear, it's not fun up there.

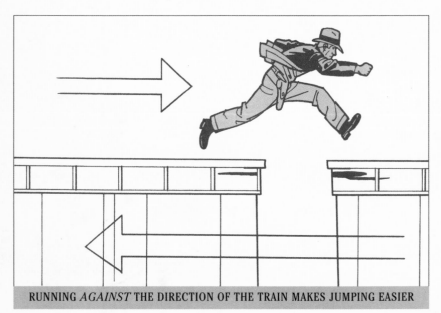

RUNNING *AGAINST* THE DIRECTION OF THE TRAIN MAKES JUMPING EASIER

6. EXITING THE TRAIN.

In Indy's day, locomotives had to stop often to take on water or coal to fuel their engines. Modern trains are powered by diesel fuel or electricity and don't have to stop unless they need to pick up freight or passengers. During the long stretches between stops, the engineers may nudge the throttle up to 100 miles per hour and beyond. You don't want to be on top of the train when that happens. When the train approaches a railyard or station, descend the ladder to the last rung, wait till the train stops, and drop off. You may be tempted to drop into a boxcar opening and ride it to your final destination. Before you do, just be sure you're not leaping into something deadly, such as a pit of live snakes.

HOW TO CROSS A ROPE BRIDGE

Rope bridges are common in many of the world's remote locations, and they are excellent examples of vernacular, or folk-based, engineering. The Incas spanned high gorges with suspension bridges fashioned from thick woven grasses. After a year or so, when these bridges began to sag in the middle, communities gathered to twirl new cables and rebuild them. This custom continues into modern times as a celebration of Inca heritage and has become a wonderful destination experience for savvy tourists. A similar bridge exists in Carrick-a-Rede, County Antrim, Ireland, a popular European destination. In general, you will find such bridges to be a good way to get around wherever you find them on your archaeological travels. Good, that is, provided they have been properly maintained, you're traveling light, and you are not being chased by sword-wielding maniacs. If that happens, you must be prepared to do the unthinkable.

1. CHECK YOUR MOORINGS.

Though it may be difficult to think straight when hostiles begin chasing you toward an inaccessible canyon, it's still a good idea to check that the cables are firmly attached to the rock pylons on your side of the bridge. Be aware that bridge materials, being organic, may be affected by the weather. In a dry season, the cables will sag less but be more brittle. In a wet season, they may be more flexible. Admittedly, there is no way to check the moorings on the other side of the span. Therefore, if you find your side to be sturdy, go for it; run as fast as you can toward the middle, taking care to hold onto the railing with both hands. Running may prove difficult if the floor of the bridge is made of woven grass. You'll step and sink, step and sink. Just lift your knees high to disentangle yourself from the webbing. At all costs, strive to stay ahead of your pursuers.

2. MONITOR CONSTRUCTION ON THE RUN.

You must be open to the possibility that the bridge is poorly constructed, or that parts of it will give way underfoot. It is, after all, a bridge made of rope. Or grass. If a small section of the floor drops away, you should be able to recover nicely by extricating your foot and stepping over the gap to a sturdier portion of the bridge. If a large section has rotted out, face the side wall of the bridge, insert the toes of your shoes into the nooks, and climb sideways until you reach safe footing.

3. BE PREPARED FOR THE WORST.

If at any time you think the structure isn't going to hold, be prepared to use your bullwhip to lash yourself to the sturdiest nearby ropes. If you prefer to reserve your bullwhip to deal with your attackers, then entwine your limbs into the ropes and hold on tight. It isn't pleasant to do, but you should look over the side to know what you're dealing with. If the bridge gives way, will you plunge into water, hit rocks, or confront ornery crocodiles? Be prepared to jettison your rucksack, if you must. Don't worry about your precious cargo. To paraphrase the infamous Mola Ram: The Sankara Stones will be found, but you won't.

4. THINK: OBSTACLES.

In such tight quarters, obstacles can become a huge hindrance. If your pursuers are gaining on you, consider obstructing the way with whatever you have handy in your rucksack. Your mess kit. A tent. A sleeping bag. Violence isn't pretty, but if you can disable one man, you may slow down the others enough to make it to the other side.

5. IF YOU MUST, CUT!

Should your attackers close in on you from both ends of the bridge, and you're running out of time, go with the one option they will never see coming: Cut the bridge. Lash yourself in quickly and hack at the ropes with

CUTTING A ROPE BRIDGE

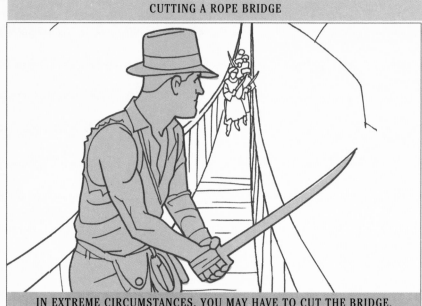

IN EXTREME CIRCUMSTANCES, YOU MAY HAVE TO CUT THE BRIDGE.

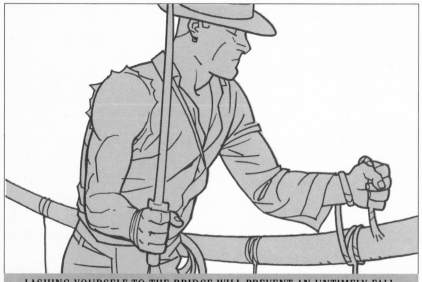

LASHING YOURSELF TO THE BRIDGE WILL PREVENT AN UNTIMELY FALL.

CUT QUICKLY AND WITHOUT HESITATION

AS THE BRIDGE COLLAPSES, SO WILL YOUR OPPONENTS.

your machete. If you must go this route, do it quickly and without hesitation. You don't want the cretins to have a chance to save themselves. When they see you raise your machete, no one will even try to stop you. Most will simply try to scamper madly off the bridge and forget to hang on to the sides. When the bridge goes, they'll be flung into the chasm below. Keep some simple geometry in mind: If you cut when you're in the middle of the bridge, you will be on the whip end and have the farthest to fall before the bridge slams into the rock walls of the gorge. The closer you are to one side when you cut, the better—provided you tie yourself to the short end of the bridge. Of course, if you're that close to the other side, whip (or shoot) your way to the other side, then send your enemies and the bridge to the bottom of the pit.

6. FIGHT YOUR WAY TO THE TOP.

Unfortunately the battle's not over when the bridge goes down. Because of that pesky geometry, you will now be at the very bottom of the remaining bridge section. At best you will be the only man left standing—er, dangling. At worst, you will have to fight your way to the top, peeling away your attackers' fingers from the ropes and sending them plunging straight into the gaping mouth of Hell. But don't start climbing just yet. Take a breather. Wait until the weaker parties lose their grip and start plummeting like stones. Then take on the stragglers. Curl your lip, pull yourself up one rung at a time, and show these rope-clinging creeps why they should never, ever mess with an archaeologist with a degree from an institution of higher learning.

MINE CARS

These vehicles are designed to carry ore, not humans. Avoid using them as transportation. If you simply must use a mine car, get into the vehicle and stay down. A human's weight distribution varies greatly from, say, a pile of coal, so the car can easily fly off the tracks if it picks up too much speed. Worse, you may be pitched out of the car. Be smart: Brace yourself by placing your back against the rear wall of the car and your legs on the front wall. If the car goes into a turn, shift your body weight in the opposite direction to balance the car. Raise your head only to check the progress of your journey. If your car is equipped with a brake, apply it gently, for the crude wooden handles do tend to break. Never linger in a mine tunnel, because the buildup of carbon dioxide and other gases can be fatal. If you can switch tracks to a clearly marked shortcut, take it. To offset the weight issue, it pays to travel with a colleague or two.

HOW TO OUT-DRIVE THE ENEMY

W hether you are trying to outrun or catch up to someone, you may find yourself needing to go beyond the regular rules of the road in order to protect life and limb, as well as any artifacts you happen to be carrying. On many occasions, Indiana Jones has found himself in the driver's seat and under attack. Driving, punching, and shooting simultaneously is not easy, but Indy has demonstrated more than once that it can be done. Such dexterity is exhausting and dangerous, and the stakes are usually high. However, there's nothing like a bumper full of armed gunmen to bring out your best behind the wheel.

1. USE YOUR SITUATION AND SURROUNDINGS.

Know your strengths and your perceived weaknesses, and use both to your advantage. This will help you make sharper on-the-spot driving decisions. If your vehicle is small and lacking the power of your pursuer, it may also be easier to maneuver through winding roads and narrow tunnels. If your car is big and unwieldy, it can still be used to ram the other vehicle(s) off the road (see step 5).

2. FIND THE ENEMY'S WEAKNESS.

Assess your pursuers' situation as well. Although you may be happy to bone up on your six-shooter skills with one hand on the wheel, it's often easier to disable the vehicle rather than the driver.

3. MAKE A SUDDEN 180-DEGREE TURN.

The following evasive turns can take you quickly in the opposite direction.

- **The J-turn or "moonshiner's turn":** This turn is ideal if you come up against a dead end and need to turn around and get out of the situation quickly. The J-turn is essentially a U-turn done in reverse. First, stop your vehicle. Start backing up and, after driving in reverse for a few seconds, slip into neutral, pull up on the emergency brake, and cut hard to the left. Ideally you will turn around 180 degrees. Then release the brake, put it in gear, and hit it.
- **The handbrake turn or "bootlegger's turn":** The momentum of the car is important here, so you need speed to pull this off—which could be tricky depending on what and where you're driving. In a

PERFORMING A J-TURN

ACCELERATE IN REVERSE WHILE CHECKING YOUR MIRRORS FOR OBSTACLES.

SHIFT INTO NEUTRAL.

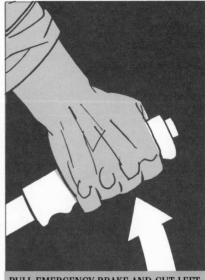

PULL EMERGENCY BRAKE AND CUT LEFT.

THE VEHICLE WILL SWING 180 DEGREES.

RELEASE BRAKE, SHIFT INTO GEAR, AND DRIVE AWAY.

simultaneous motion, shift into neutral and pull up on the emergency brake—which will cause you to skid—and immediately turn your wheel sharply to the left. Once the rear of the vehicle has stopped moving, shift back into gear and floor it.

4. SPOT AND DROP HANGERS-ON.

Keep in mind that if you are in pursuit of someone, there may be others coming after you, too. No escape in a motor vehicle will occur without bad guys creeping alongside your truck, sneaking their way along your running board, jumping into the front seat, and attempting to eject you from it. So, take a note from Driver's Ed and check your mirrors. Once spotted, these intruders can be easily disengaged with a swift swerve to the right or left. Again, being aware of your surroundings can help you brush off pesky side-board surfers. Trees, shrubs, and especially rocky protrusions can scrape off even the most stubborn cling-ons. Slamming the brakes will place the laws of momentum firmly in your favor and may even land your attackers in front of your moving vehicle, where you will have additional options for dealing with them—permanently.

5. GET UP-CLOSE AND PERSONAL.

Ramming a car off the road or out of your way is a handy option if you are in the right vehicle—but size matters. If you want to ram an SUV with a compact hybrid, you're probably out of luck. But if you have a larger vehicle than the enemy's—or if the two vehicles are the same size—this technique can work.

- If you have an airbag, you may want to disable it. You won't be able to see should it open, which will make it particularly difficult to continue driving.
- Approach the car at a 90-degree angle. If impossible, do your best.
- Increasing your speed right before impact, ram the front passenger side into either rear wheel of the target vehicle. Try to do so at as close to a 90-degree angle as possible.

If your object is to get the car out of the way or off the road, do not ram the main chassis. That will not move it far and will just anger your machine-gun-toting nemesis in the target vehicle.

6. USE PEDESTRIANS TO YOUR ADVANTAGE.

It is of the utmost importance to keep damage to pedestrians and their property to a minimum. Yet the chaos of many international cities—impossibly small streets, non-stop bazaars, spice-toting locals, creaky rickshaws—can be great diversions. Consider Short Round's heroic drive through the streets of Shanghai, in which the 11-year-old helps Indy and Miss Willie Scott evade Lao Che's henchmen.

7. HIDE IN PLAIN SIGHT.

The bustling squares and secluded side streets of many towns and cities can offer myriad options for a quick cover. A canvas or tent and some carefully positioned fruit and vegetable carts can quickly camouflage your vehicle as a top-notch vendor stand. Hide your tracks if time permits.

8. FINALLY, A WORD ABOUT STICK SHIFTS.

While outside the United States, don't expect to find many vehicles with automatic transmissions. In the eyes of the rest of the modern—and not-so-modern—world, automatics are for the infirm, those who have lost one or more limbs, and Americans. If you have never driven stick, you have few choices but to take a crash (so to speak) course before departing on your journey. Otherwise, your travel options—especially those on short notice—will be limited to the passenger seat or the saddle. (See "The Animal Kingdom," page 98, for more.)

MOTORCYCLE SIDECARS

If you are forced to travel on a motorcycle equipped with a sidecar, consider first if you really need that extra appendage. You will travel more quickly without the sidecar, which can be easily removed by detaching the metal struts. But that takes time you may not have. In case of a road chase, exploit the motorcycle's advantages over other motor vehicles. You can pull off the road and hide in the woods. You can race up dirt roads and slip through narrow passages that may be inaccessible to a truck or touring car. If your pursuers are firing weapons at you, your compatriot riding in the "hack" seat can easily return fire while you attend to navigation. If another bike is on your tail, take them out with a stout stick inserted into the spokes of their wheels. Hey, if it worked for Indy, it'll work for you.

HOW TO PASS UNDER A MOVING TRUCK

If you happen to find yourself on the wrong side of a windshield and sliding off the hood, you don't have a lot of options. The best way to regain your footing is to work with the laws of gravity and physics, and make your way underneath the vehicle. Being on the ground behind a moving truck is obviously preferable to being on the ground in front of one. This maneuver also gives you the always important element of surprise. You will seem to have disappeared under the vehicle and met an untimely, gear-gobbled end, only to reappear (relatively) unscathed and capable of catching the driver off-guard. This tactic is not ideal, but it may be the best way out of a sticky situation.

1. START OFF SLOWLY.

Passing under a truck is rarely a first choice for travelers, and your decision to do so will probably be the result of a rather unceremonious ejection from the seated area of the vehicle. Gather your composure for a few seconds—do not hurry to get under the vehicle. After all, if you're already on the hood and a degenerate with a gleam in his eye is driving, you're going to end up there one way or another.

2. GET LOW.

Lowering yourself down over the front of the vehicle slowly and method-ically will help ensure a safer passage. On your belly, allow your feet to go over the front of the vehicle first. Hold on to the hood ornament, grille, and finally the front bumper and let your feet trail under the vehicle.

3. PROTECT YOUR HANDS.

Driving gloves aren't just for driving. The underbelly of a truck chassis is a sizzling hot and steamy place, and recoiling from a burn on your hand can seriously undermine your attempts to make it through without incident.

4. MIND YOUR HEAD.

Your head should always be pointed in the direction the vehicle is moving. That will allow you to concentrate on protecting your noggin and keeping your hat on. Your feet will simply drag along the ground as the car moves forward. Well, not *simply*. It may smart a bit. We can't say enough about good boots (see "How to Pack for an Expedition," page 18).

5. MOVE QUICKLY BUT CALMLY TOWARD THE REAR OF THE TRUCK.

As you make your way along the underside of the truck chassis, try to move as quickly as possible without compromising your grip. Grab the frame of the truck and keep away from moving parts. The drive shaft may look tempting, since it provides a one-way direct route to the other end of the vehicle, but it rotates—and that could get messy. Also keep in mind that some of the parts may be hot, even with gloves; you will be motivated to move on in a timely fashion. Focus on keeping your arms in as close to your body as possible to consolidate your center of gravity. As you near your goal, be sure to keep your head clear of the gear box or "pumpkin" between the rear axles.

6. GET HOOKED.

When you're ready to make your exit from under the vehicle, latch your bullwhip onto some fixed part of the chassis. *Fixed* is the key word here. Wrapping your bull whip around a turning axle is a guaranteed way to end up face-to-face with the transmission. If you can attach your bullwhip to a hook and attach the hook to the chassis, that will work even better and cut down on tangling issues. Be sure that as you use one hand to attach the whip, your other hand is still holding on to the vehicle.

7. COMPLETE THE PASS.

Before letting go and careening your way along the ground toward the rear of the vehicle, be sure that the length of your bullwhip is greater than the distance from the point of attachment to the back of the vehicle. The goal here is to make sure that your head will clear the bumper; you don't want to land looking up at the muffler. Once you're reasonably sure that your starting position is far enough along the underside of the vehicle, grab onto the bullwhip with both hands and let yourself be carried along the ground until the bullwhip is taut and you have cleared the rear of the vehicle. Roll onto your stomach as you exit so you can see what's going on around you.

BEFORE RELEASING YOUR BULLWHIP, CHECK BEHIND YOU FOR ONCOMING VEHICLES.

8. CHOOSE YOUR NEXT PLAY.

At this point, you are being dragged behind a moving truck. Although this doesn't sound very appealing, after spending the last few minutes under the truck it should be a somewhat welcome relief. You now have two choices: You can let go of the bullwhip and end your journey right then and there. This choice is impractical if you have any devotion whatsoever to your task at hand, which is to get hold of the cretins driving off with valuable artifacts or information. It is also not the wisest choice if another vehicle is coming up behind you.

Or, you can use your well-toned biceps to work your way, hand-over-hand, along the length of the whip until you reach the bumper and pull yourself back onto the vehicle.

HOW TO FLY A PLANE

Whether you are abandoned at high altitudes or desperately need to exit a zeppelin—always a good idea, considering their track record—the situation may arise when you find yourself behind the controls of an airplane, perhaps for the first time. Don't panic. Flying a plane is not that difficult. (Landing it is another matter entirely. See page 56.) Here are the basics.

- **Look around.** Notice if you are flying straight or if your wings are rising and falling erratically.
- **Every plane has a steering wheel,** just like a car. It's called a yoke, and it's just where you would imagine it—right in front of you. And guess what? It turns the plane. It also controls the pitch, which is how much the nose of the plane is pointing down or up. Pull back to raise the nose of the plane, push forward to lower it. While cruising, you want to keep the nose of the plane about three inches (or 75 millimeters) below the horizon.
- **Check the fuel gauge.** It should be located in the lower portion of the instrument panel. If you have fuel, great. If you don't, you may want to go ahead and skip down to the sections on when to bail (page 58) and how to survive a plane crash (page 59).
- **Find the altimeter.** It will tell you what your altitude is. Like a clock, it has a big hand and a small hand; the big hand indicates altitude in hundreds of feet above sea level, and the small hand in thousands of feet. Of course, as a scientist and well-seasoned traveler, you

should be prepared for kilometers and meters, the standard of meas-
urement used by, well, everyone else in the world.

- **Check your heading, or direction.** There is a compass on the
instrument panel that will have the image of a small plane in the
middle of it. It will tell you in which direction you're headed.

- **Check your speed.** It should be on the upper part of the panel,
toward the left. The speed will likely be in knots. Cruising at 120
knots is a nice speed for a small plane. If you're going less than 70
knots, you have a major problem and may soon find yourself a victim of gravity. Speed up.

- **Your throttle controls your speed** and the relation of the nose to
the horizon. It is located to the right of your seat and looks vaguely like
the gear shift on some standard transmission cars. Push it forward to
speed up and ascend, pull back on it to slow down and descend.

LANDING A PLANE

You may be able to wing it, so to speak, when attempting to fly a plane that
is already airborne and in no immediate need to land. But bringing the bird
down in a manner that leaves you—if not the plane—intact is a little trickier. It may happen that, in the course of escape or pursuit, you are tempted
to fly a plane without actually thinking about how you might land it. That
doesn't demonstrate the greatest amount of foresight, but hey—sometimes
you have to make things up as you go along.

If you're lucky enough to be in a plane with a radio headset, put it on.
Push to talk, and release to listen. The button will be on either the instrument
panel or the steering wheel (the yoke, remember?). If you get someone with
a pulse and more than two brain cells on the other end, explain your situation: You're an eminent, widely published archaeologist who had no other
choice but to get behind the wheel of a plane and fly it, despite that you know

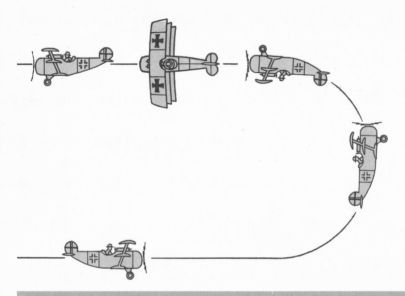

IF YOU ARE BEING PURSUED, THE IMMELMAN TURN (OR I-TURN) IS AN EFFECTIVE WAY TO EVADE THE ENEMY.

nothing about how to land it. Follow their instructions, assuming, that is, that they speak English, Latin, or ancient Greek.

But, you probably won't be that lucky. If you have no choice but to land the plane yourself, try the following:

- Pick a nice spot to land, but don't get too picky; you probably won't have the luxury of time. Your choice of landing site will likely be limited. An open field is the best option, but any large, flat, uninterrupted stretch of land will do.
- Pull back on the throttle. That will slow the plane and drop the nose for the descent. Try to keep the nose about four inches (or 10 cm) below the horizon. If in a small plane, try to maintain a speed of about 90 knots.

- Lower the landing gear. On some small planes, the gear may be fixed, and you're in luck. If not, the lever should be near the throttle, and it is shaped like a tire.

- When you are approaching the landing site, reduce the power even more by pulling back on the throttle. Do not let the nose drop more than six inches (15 cm) below the horizon.

- The plane should be about 100 feet off the ground when you are above your landing site. You want the rear wheels to hit first. At about 70 knots the plane will enter the stalling zone, and that's where you want to be when you land.

- Pull way back on the throttle, but not so much that your nose dips too deeply. As the plane touches the ground, pull back gently— GENTLY—on the yoke.

- On the ground, the yoke will be of little use to you. Now it's all up to your feet. There are two sets of pedals: upper pedals and lower pedals. The lower pedals control the plane's nose, turning it right or left. If you are about to crash into a barn or a crowd of innocent bystanders, these are your only hope. The upper pedals are for the brakes.

- Slow down. You drastically increase your chances of survival if you do.

WHEN TO BAIL

Sometimes bailing out is not only the best option—it's the only option. Should you suddenly wake from your in-flight snooze to discover that the only other living creatures on board, aside from your somewhat inept travel companions, are a bunch of clucking, feather-flapping fowl and that you're flying on fumes, you may wish to make for the door. (If you'd rather take your chances and ride it out to the bumpy end, see below.) If the pilot and the other charming individuals who left you alone on board careening toward imminent death absconded with all the parachutes—as disreputable hired-killer types are wont to do—your only option may be an inflatable raft or emergency slide. Choose this option if you are flying over water or snow. If you do, in fact, go with the raft, try to distribute your weight as evenly as possible during your descent to help prevent the raft from flipping end over end. If you are flying over land with no water in sight, it's better to stay with the plane.

SURVIVING A PLANE CRASH

Not to focus on the negative here, but if you have taken it upon yourself to fly a plane without any prior training whatsoever, you may be about to crash-land. Here are some techniques to minimize the potentially catastrophic effects of meeting the ground at high speed:

- Always travel in long pants, long-sleeved shirts, and closed-toe, sturdy shoes. Most of these items were covered in the packing list and are generally a good idea on any expedition, since they protect the majority of your skin. Natural fibers are best, since they won't melt into your epidermis like synthetic fibers will.
- If you have a seatbelt, make sure it's fastened. If you don't, well, hope for the best.
- Brace your feet or knees against the object in front of you.
- Place your head in your lap and protect it with a soft object. A folded bomber jacket will do nicely in a pinch.
- Stay calm and relaxed. Seriously. It's your best bet for survival.
- Wait until the plane has stopped before exiting and do so as quickly as possible, since the craft may burst into flames. Do not take any luggage or personal belongings—except for irreplaceable diaries, rubbings of ancient texts, or valuable artifacts. After all, you just survived a plane crash. Why give up now?

ROCKET SLEDS

Should you find yourself pursued by enemy agents across barren government facilities, rocket sleds may prove to be, as one did for Indy, an excellent way to evade capture. Rocket sleds are scientific instruments, not conventional transportation. They are used to test, among other things, the human response to incredible speeds, the efficacy of ejection seats, and the design of parachutes without the added complication of sending a human pilot into air or space. The rocket-powered, sled-like vehicle clamps onto railroad-like tracks, and—when reaching speeds faster than 200 miles per hour with g-force fifteen times more powerful than that of a roller-coaster—actually glides on a cushion of air above the track. This is truly frictionless travel. Unfortunately, there's rarely a windshield, so your body will probably be battered by air at all times. Keep your wits about you, and always wear goggles. In early rocket-sled tests, one rider burst all the capillaries in his eyeballs. Another pilot, Captain E. A. Murphy, is remembered as the originator of Murphy's Law: "Whatever can go wrong, will." You might want to consider that maxim before hopping aboard this sucker.

HOW TO ESCAPE QUICKSAND

Quicksand exists wherever underground streams or rivers have flowed upward, turning sandy soil into a liquefied mush. The danger posed by quicksand is a little like falling into a large body of water—with one crucial difference: Quicksand doesn't let go. Molecules of water break easily when you tug against them. Sand's tendency is to stick with other sand, and it's hard to break the vacuum. Despite this, it's still easy to extricate yourself from quicksand, provided you follow a few simple rules.

1. DON'T PANIC.

As in water, kicking and thrashing only makes matters worse. With each kick, you are digging a hole for your body to descend. If you stop moving entirely, your body will actually float to the surface. That's because the density of a human body is less than the surrounding quicksand liquid.

2. JETTISON HEAVY BELONGINGS.

Your rucksack, backpack, and laptop are working against your chances of survival. Strip them off your back and shoulders while you still have use of your arms, and keep clear of the straps. If you simply cannot afford to lose the contents of your pack, pitch it to dry land. Understand that forceful throwing movements can embed you further.

ESCAPING QUICKSAND

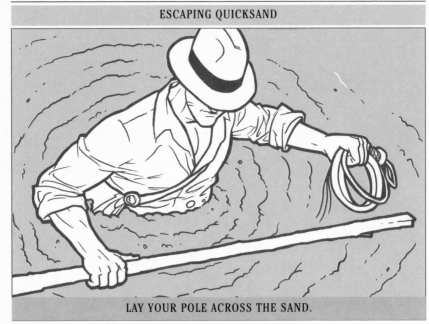

LAY YOUR POLE ACROSS THE SAND.

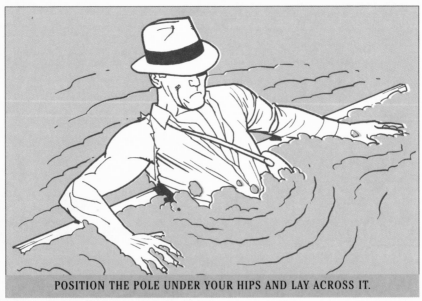

POSITION THE POLE UNDER YOUR HIPS AND LAY ACROSS IT.

WRAP YOUR WHIP AROUND A NEARBY TREE.

PULL YOURSELF TO SAFETY.

3. MOVE SLOWLY.

The sand will release you eventually, as long as you don't struggle against it. Some explorers have s-l-o-w-l-y swum out of quicksand, but it may take an hour to go a dozen feet. Others have had success letting the sand carry them to the surface, then flopping gently onto their backs. Whatever you do, do it at a glacier's pace. Let the sand slowly ebb back and replace what you have pulled from it. It will be tiring to work against the suction. One way to overcome the pull is to always travel with a stout pole, thick rope, or your trusty bullwhip. At the first sign of danger, lay the pole horizontally across the sand, and stay still until you naturally float to the surface. Lie back across the pole and position it under your hips, perpendicular to your body. That will keep your hips—most people's center of gravity—from sinking. Toss a rope or wrap your bullwhip around a stationary object just outside the sinking pool, and pull yourself to safety. Just remember that extracting your bullwhip from your belt will be difficult if your hips have already sunk below the surface.

4. PUT COLLEAGUES IN THEIR PLACE.

A colleague on shore can be of great assistance, provided he keeps his cool. It does you no good to have someone shouting, "Quick, grab the rope! Do it now!" They may not understand that you are better off moving slowly and cannot instantly respond to their instructions. So, as soon as you can, speak loudly but calmly to them. Let them know that you are not ignoring them, just moving slowly but deliberately toward their assistance. This is yet another example of how good communication skills can keep an expedition running smoothly.

5. ANTICIPATE SOLID GROUND.

Most pools of quicksand are not deep. It's possible that your feet will hit solid ground after you sink waist deep, and you can easily propel yourself forward or walk to shore on this hard layer. If so, consider yourself lucky. But bear in mind that as you move to shore, all previous rules apply. The hard ground might drop off suddenly or turn to mush. You don't want to lose your balance and fall head first into the muck.

HOW TO SURVIVE FOR SEVERAL DAYS CLINGING TO A SUBMARINE'S PERISCOPE

It's easy to trail suspects, looters, or undesirables when they're speeding away in a motor vehicle. Just hop in your set of wheels and give chase. Heck, you could even pursue them on a horse. But how do you follow your man when his getaway vehicle of choice is a submarine? Thankfully, Indiana Jones has already shed light on pulling off this tricky feat. While pursuing arch rival Rene Belloq to a remote island (where Belloq had brought the kidnapped Marion Ravenwood and planned to open the Ark of the Covenant), Dr. Jones had no choice but to leap overboard from the tramp steamer *Bantu Wind*, which had been boarded by German troops. At that point, Jones's only option to get to the island was to stow away on—not in—an enemy submarine. Here's how he did it.

1. DIVE IN—NOW.

The biggest trick in a submarine's arsenal is its invisibility. If it drops completely underwater, it's lost to you forever. So, the second you hear the klaxon sound and the captain shout, "Dive!" jump in the ocean and swim toward the boat. Aim for the sail, which is the tall, vertical part of the submarine that rises from its horizontal, cigar-shaped hull. In vintage subs, this part houses the periscope and the snorkel, a vertical tube that allowed the diesel-powered engines to suck in air for combustion. In modern subs, the sail holds much of the vessel's important devices for electronic communication. You rarely see a periscope on modern subs. Why? Well, you can't see that far with them anyway, and they're a dead giveaway to enemy spotters. Whatever it takes, swim to the sail and grab hold of whatever sticks out: the periscope, the snorkel, the railing of the bridge—anything.

2. MONITOR THE SUB'S DIVE.

Submerged submarines consume more energy and resources than submarines that propel themselves along the surface. For this reason, the sub may not drop completely below the surface unless absolutely necessary— that is, when it anticipates a threat or a target ship. As the vessel pulls away, wait to see what it intends to do. If it doesn't submerge, you're golden. Hug the periscope (or whatever you are using as a support) and get ready for the ride of your life. If the sub dives partially, reach for your bullwhip.

3. LASH YOURSELF TO THE PERISCOPE.

Holding onto the periscope with one hand, use the other hand to tie your torso to it. It won't be easy tying a thick leather cord with one hand, but that's just the kind of skill you might want to practice on a Friday night while taking a break from your studies. Don't get fancy or complicated. The knot must hold fast and still come loose when you give it a tug. Before you tie yourself in, make sure you're in a comfortable position to breathe easily, even in the wake of the water caused by the sub's maneuvers. You must be high enough to breathe even if you should, say, fall asleep.

4. KNOW WHAT TO EXPECT.

Who are we kidding? This is no picnic, but time and technology are, arguably, on your side. A vintage submarine can stay submerged only about 60 or 70 miles, and they travel only about 4 knots, or 9 miles per hour. Totally dealable. A modern submarine, sorry to say, can cruise underwater about 23 miles an hour and may even be capable of kicking it up to 46

LASH YOURSELF TO THE PERISCOPE WITH YOUR BULLWHIP.

miles per hour. Piece of cake, you say? Here comes the bad news: Unlike their WWII counterparts, they can stay submerged for 8,000 miles at a time. So if you're going to take on a sub, make it easy on yourself and pick an old warhorse. If you think you'll be underwater for a while, it doesn't hurt to trap some air in your clothes. Simply raise your jacket out of the ocean and bring it down on the water to form an air pocket. This will give you a few mouthfuls of air to use in a pinch. Just remember to use clothing that is fairly thick, such as a leather bomber jacket.

5. BE DEEP-DIVE-READY.

On the frightening off-chance that the vessel decides to completely submerge itself underwater, you have two choices: Bail immediately or go to Plan B. Lash the sturdy end of your bullwhip to the tallest possible point of the sub, hold tight to the other end of the whip, and release your arms and legs from the periscope. The force of the water will carry you up, and you'll be able to ride along after the sub, albeit from the surface of the sea. This is not preferable, of course, since you are slightly more vulnerable at sea without a sturdy strut on which to hang your hat, not to mention yourself. If the sub dives deeper, tie some rope from your rucksack to the end of your bullwhip and pay out the rope gently, as needed. Just know that while WWII-era subs can dive only about 656 feet, modern subs can descend twice that distance. Pack a long rope.

ZEPPELINS

Invented in 1900 by Count Ferdinand von Zeppelin, these rigid dirigibles fly by virtue of a massive "balloon" shell that is filled with still smaller cells that are filled with helium gas. The tragic 1937 Hindenburg incident doomed a technology that was, until that time, regarded as a safe and luxurious way to fly. It is highly unlikely that you will need to ride a zeppelin in the course of your travels, though zeppelins are used today for tourist excursions and occasional academic research. As always, if you have created enemies in the course of your travels, be prepared to jump ship. Pack a parachute, obey all safety regulations as you would aboard an ordinary commercial flight, and please, whatever you do, keep your ticket with you at all times.

CHAPTER 3

PEOPLE SKILLS

As an archaeologist, you are charged with not only researching and collecting artifacts from other cultures but also putting those artifacts within the proper cultural and ethnographic context. While on expedition you will be interacting, competing, and sometimes even fighting with local people to get where you're going and what you need.

In addition to language skills, an understanding of customs and habits is indispensable, as is the ability to get along with (or fend off) others. These skills can be life-savers, whether you are attempting to surreptitiously obtain information at a dinner party in India or to get assistance in deciphering markings on an ancient medallion. The better you adhere to local custom, the more smoothly your encounters will proceed.

HOW TO BLEND IN

W hen in Rome," goes the saying, "do as the Romans do." The original speaker of these lines was undoubtedly Roman, but he had a point. You don't want to appear like museum curator Marcus Brody, wandering the street bazaars of life in a white linen suit, asking if anyone speaks English. If your work takes you to different lands, then you must learn to deftly vanish into the cultures of those lands. Knowing how to do so effectively can save your life on those unfortunate occasions when you have run afoul of the local warlord, maniacal millionaire, or international madman. The line between "blending" and "hiding" is often a fine one. There may be times when you want to disappear in plain sight to gain access to a particular site without attracting attention. And there may be times when you simply cannot risk being seen, period.

1. LEARN THE LANGUAGE.

We cannot stress this enough. Bone up on the language using whatever means are at your disposal: audio CDs, textbooks, and phrasebooks. We know: Hovitos phrasebooks show up so rarely in bookstores. And yes, it is hard to master a foreign tongue. But so is extricating yourself from the clutches of a tyrannical tribal chief who believes you just insulted his mother when you really meant to compliment him on his festive headgear.

2. DRESS THE PART.

You might think you're a chic, original dresser, but most people in the world will peg you as a Westerner and an American, to boot. If you need to blend, adopt the dress of your host country. In the Middle East, for example, that will probably mean wearing a thobe, a gutra, and sandals (see examples on page 75). The more voluminous your garments, the more easily you will be able to shield your face. A dark-complexioned man who tans well can easily grow out his beard, don these garments, and blend easily. If you're fairer, consider traveling with an instant-tan lotion and a set of dark contact lenses. And ditch any backpacks or briefcases you may be carrying. They brand you as an American—and a dork. Observe what the locals use to carry their gear, and outfit yourself accordingly.

3. ACT THE PART.

Speaking and dressing are only part of the story. You must imitate the body language, gestures, behavior, and even the gait of ordinary people around you. If you're wearing a sari but walking like a Westerner, you'll look like a Westerner wearing a sari. Mimic the way others move, but don't overdo it. Eat what is served to you without complaint. Make yourself look useful. Carry something—a cage of chickens, a rolled-up carpet, a terra-cotta jug of water—and others will believe you belong there.

4. MOVE IN LARGE GROUPS.

There's safety and confusion in numbers. If you need to get from a train station to a hotel, for example, tag along with a group of farmers bringing their goods to market. Anyone trying to spot you will be looking for a single person traveling alone, and they won't look twice at a gaggle of noisy commoners.

5. WEAR A UNIFORM.

Under the right circumstances, an authority figure blends into the woodwork as easily as a laborer laying bricks. When was the last time you looked a cop in the eye? If you have no choice and the bad guys are closing in, clunk a guard, soldier, or other official on the head, and take his uniform. There are only two major rules to remember: Stash the unconscious lug somewhere where he won't foil your plan, and make sure you take on someone your own size. A soldier in flood pants? That people would notice.

6. CULTIVATE FAR-FLUNG FRIENDS.

It helps to have as many native-born foreign friends as possible in various outposts of the world. Should you find yourself in Cairo, for instance, it helps to have someone like Sallah, Indy's Egyptian chum, to grease the skids, arrange transportation, run interference, and steer you away from bad dates. Friendship is not networking. Forget snagging a bunch of business cards at the next archaeology conference and then ringing your new "pals" for favors.

Embedded chums are rare. If Indy didn't have Sallah, he would have never been able to hitch a ride with the cargo pirates when he was chasing the lost Ark. So treasure these compatriots, wherever you are, and you will always have help slipping in the back door of a distant land.

IF YOU NEED TO BLEND IN, WEAR A UNIFORM OR ADOPT THE DRESS OF YOUR HOST COUNTRY.

KNOW YOUR GREETING CUSTOMS

In Western societies, it's common to shake hands upon greeting someone. This custom is rooted in the ancient practice of grasping another's hands to be certain he is not bearing weapons. A familiarity with greeting customs gets things off on the right foot. For example, in a span of 48 hours, Indy has found himself switching deftly from doing business in cosmopolitan Shanghai to exchanging greetings with the village Shaman of Mayapore. The following are greetings in other cultures.

- In China, people may applaud upon meeting you. Don't be alarmed. Just smile and gently clap back.
- In Egypt, shake hands with your acquaintance, and then gently touch the person's elbow.
- In India, join your hands together at the chest, dip your head, and utters the word "Namaste," which means, "I salute you." The same is done upon departure, either with or without words to indicate the same things.
- In Italy, revert to your knowledge of Latin. Greet Romans with "Salve." Though popular in the U.S., never say "Ciao"— "hello" and "goodbye"—to someone who is not an intimate friend. The proper term is "Arrivederci," the more formal "Arrivederla" (goodbye), or "Buon giorno/Buona sera" (good day/evening).

- In Japan, bow from the waist to greet and say farewell. Your bow should match your friend's bow in duration and depth. This is tricky; if you can, observe the other party and tailor yours to match his or hers. (Buddhists, however, use a gesture, called the gassho, which is similar to the Indian "Namaste.")

- In many South American nations, the abrazo—or embrace—is a common hello. Men throw their arms around each other and give each other a few light taps on the back; women hug and kiss the air beside each other's cheeks. Another variant in Latin culture is to lock and shake each other's forearms.

- In nations where Arabic is spoken, use "Salaam" ("peace") to greet people.

- In Persia, you may be expected to greet children with a handshake to demonstrate respect for their parents. Watch for this practice, and do the same.

HOW TO HANDLE AWKWARD FOODS

We've all been there: An uncomfortable dinner party where you struggle to down the evening's fare, too polite to tell the host or hostess that they should have coughed up the extra dough for a caterer. Or perhaps you've spent years unable to tell your mother that the "secret family recipe" she's so proud of, the one she serves at every holiday from Thanksgiving to Arbor Day, should, in fact, remain a secret and perhaps be buried with her.

We all need food to survive, and it can arouse either our passions or our bile with the same ease. Eating can sometimes make you feel as though you are taking your life into your own hands. As you travel to distant and sometimes obscure corners of the world, you may find yourself on interesting and involuntary culinary adventures. From grasshoppers to head cheese, every culture has its most and least favorite treats. One man's delicacy is another man's nausea, and it is important to keep an open mind and roll with the gastronomical punches in order to be respectful to your hosts and companions.

It's also important to remember that meals—and especially dinner parties—can be an ideal setting for gathering information, as long as you're subtle enough to hide the fact that you are doing so. While dining with the Maharaja at Pankot Palace, Indiana Jones pushed the limits of his disconcertingly charming host, Chattar Lal, by hinting at the palace's role in keeping the power of the dark light alive and well, all the while acting as though

CULTIVATE A TASTE FOR STRANGE AND EXOTIC MEALS.

it were nothing more than captivating dinner patter. Unfortunately, his lack of subtlety earned him an unwanted sip of the blood of the Kali, which caused him to fall into the dark sleep of the Kali Ma. Therefore, we will reiterate the importance of being respectful of your hosts, even if they are attempting to revive the popularity of a long-dead cult of blood-drinking, heart-stealing, human-sacrificing thugs.

It's not always easy to stare down a bowl of eyeballs, a plate of intestines, or larvae pâté without as much as a wince, but it can make your stay go more smoothly. These tips may help:

1. BE MENTALLY PREPARED.

If you are attending a dinner in a remote locale, don't expect to hear "Chicken or fish?" Your expectations won't be dashed if you have lowered them appropriately. You may wish to put a little something in your stomach before sitting down to eat. Who knows? Once dinner is served, you may be pleasantly surprised. However, be forewarned: Any dish actually called "surprise" usually is—and not a pleasant one.

2. DON'T DRAW ATTENTION TO YOURSELF.

The best way to ensure your dining experience goes smoothly—especially if you're anticipating a not-so-tasty meal—is to start off by maintaining a low profile. If you can manage to be invisible, yet polite, it will also make it that much easier to inconspicuously spit food into your napkin.

3. FOCUS ON THE POSITIVE.

As live eels are released from the body of a giant snake and your fellow diners begin snacking on them, don't focus on the slimy. Think instead about the unquestionable freshness. Feel free to compliment your host with something like, "How wonderful! At home my eels are usually frozen." There will undoubtedly be some form of bread available, a good way to start your dining adventure, and one that will provide a starchy coating for your stomach. There may also be fruit offered at some point in the meal; it is a common sight on banquet tables in virtually all corners of the world. The fruits may be new and strange to you, but consider the alternative. As long as you are eating *something,* others will be less likely to ask you why you are not eating anything else.

4. MASK YOUR DISGUST AND MOVE ON.

As the food is served, be prepared to look nonplussed. Have your poker face ready before the lid comes off the platter, and do your best to keep it there. Trying to graciously defer by stating, "I had bugs for lunch," will not suffice, even if you are a famous American lounge singer from Shanghai. No matter how polite you try to be, in most dining settings it is simply not acceptable or advisable to refuse what is given to you. Be especially considerate when being hosted by those less fortunate than you are, as any food they offer represents a great sacrifice.

5. USE MIND OVER MATTER.

The mind is a remarkable tool, capable of turning frogs into princes and placebos into cure-alls. For this reason, the mind can also be a powerful ally when trying to down exotic foods that you believe belong in a terrarium instead of a chafing dish. When the eyeballs pop out of the soup, just try to think of something similar but more palatable. The vitreous humor of the eye, for example, is quite jelly-like. So try to think of, well, jelly. And don't be thrown by the presentation. Just because the eels came bursting out of a snake's belly doesn't change the fact that eel is not an uncommon snack on many continents, especially for anyone who eats sushi. Focus on what's familiar to you and not what contains it. It is much more difficult to convince yourself that monkey brains are something else when you're staring into that furry little face with the glazed-over, lifeless eyes.

6. CONSIDER YOUR HOSTS' SITUATION.

While in the Indian village of Mayapore, Indy was offered an unpalatable mush that he ate *sans* grimace. He understood that his hosts had made a tremendous sacrifice to serve him more food than they had eaten in a week. It would have been disrespectful to refuse. Whenever you are invited to dinner, be open to the social standing of your hosts and adjust your reactions accordingly. Rich or poor, a host deserves the benefit of the doubt.

7. IF YOU MUST, POLITELY ASK TO USE THE RESTROOM.

Should you believe that your best efforts to maintain your composure are about to come to a quick and potentially messy end, your last resort is to ask to be excused and use the restroom. This is preferable to passing out. Casually remarking, "Save some for me!" as you get up adds a nice touch.

ANCIENT ORDERS AND SECRET SOCIETIES

The Illuminati. The Freemasons. The Rosicrucians. History is filled with examples of secret fellowship societies. Most of these organizations are benign entities. But you must be prepared to confront dangerous and fanatical cults. Indiana Jones has battled at least two such orders.

The first, in 1935, was a revival of the Hindu cult of Thuggees, a network of thieves known for befriending, then strangling, travelers. How many Indian citizens they killed in their heyday—the 1600s to the mid-1800s—is unknown, but estimates run as high as two million. Some regard them as history's first example of organized crime. Their killings were highly ritualized, and they happily devoted a portion of their spoils to their patron, Kali, or Kali-Ma, a Hindu goddess regarded as both destroyer and creator. Stamped out by British rule in the 1830s, the Thuggees reappear as the bad guys in numerous works of Western literature, such as Gunga Din by Rudyard Kipling, Around the World in Eighty Days by Jules Verne, and a Sherlock Holmes story by Sir Arthur Conan Doyle. Though you may never have heard of Thuggees before Indy's adventure, the sect bequeathed to the English language a word you have almost certainly used: thug.

Indy's second secret society encounter, in 1938, was with the Brotherhood of the Cruciform Sword. This group of latter-day knights swears to protect the Holy Grail. Members' chests are tattooed with the same cross-like symbol Indy found emblazoned on a grail tablet and on the shield of the dead knight in the Venetian cata-combs. Though their tattoos are often hidden under their clothing, adherents are often easily identified: They always wear a stylish fez, regardless of season or occasion.

HOW TO WIN A FISTFIGHT

It's not uncommon that in your search for fact and fortune you will make more than a few enemies. Though quick with a whip and fast out of the holster, Indiana Jones has had moments that required him to get down to brass tacks and bare knuckles. When you're in a bind and without your trusty whip or pistol, knowing how to land—and, more often than not, take—a punch is a skill you will want to master. Here are some general strategies to keep in mind.

1. KNOW YOUR OPPONENT.

Do not underestimate them. It may seem obvious that the 6'4" guy with the biceps like cantaloupes who doesn't flinch when you land a right cross on his chin will be a tough challenge, but don't assume that the 5'7" guy who rarely makes a peep will be a total pushover. Although it's true that having a bit of swagger and confidence can be a big advantage in a fight, don't be so pleased with yourself and your abilities that you are blinded to the abilities—and possible advantages—of your opponent.

2. STRIKE FIRST.

It may sound trite, but getting in the first strike can often give you the advantage, especially if that punch is well-placed and directed at a pressure point. The knees, in particular, are an easy target for the small of stature. A quick hit might provide you with the advantage of crucial moments to prepare to strike again . . . or run.

3. TAKE IT OR BLOCK IT.

No one wants to get clocked. However, lunging back or to the side to avoid a punch will place you off-balance. Once you are off-balance, you are even more vulnerable to the next uppercut coming from your attacker. Any reputable tough guy will know that and will no doubt take advantage of it. A basic block, whether your opponent is aiming at the lower or upper half of your body, may keep you protected without sacrificing your footing. And if you have to take a few to the chin, so be it. It lets your attacker know that you can take whatever they can dish out . . . at least for a while.

4. HARNESS MOMENTUM TO CONSERVE ENERGY.

When it comes to scrapping in the streets, physics can be your best friend. Momentum can give you some extra power to redirect at your attacker. The best part—and one that's important to remember—is that momentum is not just generated from your own movement. The key to success is har-

PUNCHING POINTERS

GETTING IN THE FIRST PUNCH CAN GIVE YOU AN ADVANTAGE.

BASIC BLOCKS WILL PROTECT YOU WITHOUT SACRIFICING YOUR FOOTING.

IT'S BETTER TO TAKE A FEW HITS THAN FIND YOURSELF OFF-BALANCE.

A WELL-DIRECTED PUNCH CAN TAKE OUT TWO IN ONE BLOW.

nessing your opponent's energy as well; redirecting your opponent's lunges, for example, can turn the tables effectively. But don't forget to use your own momentum, especially when dealing with multiple attackers. Indy once socked two thugs with just one punch. Now that's getting the most bang for your slugging buck.

5. USE WEAKNESSES AS STRENGTHS.

Not everything that initially appears to be a weakness is a weakness. For example, if you're significantly smaller than your opponent, remember that you can move more quickly and that you have a lower center of gravity. Also, your opponent may underestimate you—if you're lucky. When attacked by the Thuggees and voodoo curses, Short Round landed some hits of his own and helped Indy gain the upper hand, despite his size. In short, always maintain your mental edge.

6. BE AWARE OF YOUR SURROUNDINGS.

Your environment can be a help or a hindrance. While trying to steal a plane and escape Tanis, Indy encountered a very large, very angry, very bald henchman who was determined to get between Indy and his way out. The goon thought he had Indy handily beat, and he was so thrilled with his own physical superiority that he didn't notice he was standing between Indy and an airplane propeller. Ouch.

HOW TO FEND OFF A GANG
OF SWORDSMEN

S o you were aces on your fencing team at university. Well, bully for you. Do not let that ivory tower smugness blind you to the fact that there are people in other parts of the world who have been working with swords from the moment they mastered their baby bottles. So don't get cocky. And remember—in sportsmanlike competition, fights are one-on-one and it is generally frowned upon to kill your opponent. However, if you are getting in the way of a hired swordsman's duty, he will not hesitate to julienne your appendages and send you packing—permanently. You have two options: Stand your ground and take your chances, or get the heck outta Dodge. If you opt to fend off your attackers, best of luck. Here are some pointers.

1. CRACK THE WHIP.

There are two primary ways in which you can use your bullwhip. The first involves keeping your attackers at a distance. A few well-placed cracks of the whip can do a lot to save your skin and buy you time to look for an escape. If your attackers can't get within a sword's length of you, you're in good shape. The other option you have at your disposal depends on your level of proficiency with your bullwhip (see "How to Use Your Bullwhip," page 24). If you have become comfortable with using your bullwhip to target specific items or individuals, you can use it to disarm your opponent. The best time to strike is when he is holding his sword with only one hand, rather than two, because it will be easier for you to snatch it from his grip. Once you have latched on to the sword with your whip, do your best to retrieve it. This may not always be possible. If it is, you will have both a sword and a bullwhip at your disposal. If it is not possible to actually get your hands on the sword, do your best to fling it as far as possible from the angry, disarmed man snarling in front of you.

2. WATCH FOR VULNERABILITIES.

It may be hard to keep your wits about you when faced with a scimitar-wielding maniac, but he, too, has his soft spots—namely, right below the sternum. Though the sight of that gleaming sword held high above your attacker's head, ready to come down and split you like a ripe melon, may rightly terrify you, it also provides opportunity. It is in this moment that the attacker's abdomen is completely exposed and his balance is more unstable than when his hands and sword are at his sides. Use this opportunity to administer a swift punch to the gut. When he doubles over, attempt to relieve him of his sword or strike him on the back of the skull.

3. GATHER SOME MOMENTUM—THEIRS.

The power that goes into a life-ending swing of a sword carries with it a lot of momentum. You can use that to your advantage. After your opponents have swung at you—and, hopefully, missed—carry or push them to continue in the same direction of their swing. Momentum will be taking them in that direction anyway, so an added shove will land them in the dirt

IF YOU'RE OUTMANNED, USE A SWORD *AND* A WHIP TO DEFEND YOURSELF.

or send them sailing over a fruit cart. If you are in the unfortunate position of having to take on more than one swordsman at a time, this technique can also be used to kill two birds with one swing. If you can, redirect the momentum of one swordsman to shove him directly into the other. If done effectively, you may be able to topple both of them and give yourself a head start.

4. USE THE CROWD.

It is never a good idea to use innocent bystanders as shields. However, they can be used to put both distance and confusion between you and the sadist with the sword. Most respectable hired assassins will not try to hack their way through those uninvolved in their quarrel, and having numerous people and animals in the wake of your escape will make it difficult for them to properly maneuver an unwieldy sword.

5. KNOW WHEN TO RUN.

If you are highly outnumbered, your smarts are your best ally. Run, and run fast. If escaping on foot, seek a crowded, bustling area. Markets are an excellent choice, allowing you to overturn numerous carts and baskets as you make your way farther and farther into the chaos. When you think you've lost your pursuers, double back. Alternatively, you could lead them down a deserted street, duck into a darkened alley or doorway, and lie in wait to make a surprise attack.

6. GET REAL.

If you find yourself face-to-face with a highly superior swordsman or a professional fighter—an opponent with no discernible weaknesses who will stop at nothing to separate you from your cerebellum—you have but one logical, life-preserving choice: Shoot him.

HOW TO BREAK FREE IF YOU ARE TIED UP

So you're tied up and left alone in a castle on the Austrian-German border? Congratulations! It could be worse. You could be handcuffed. You could be eyeing a cobra. You could be riddled with bullets and lying at the bottom of a moat. Whenever adversaries take pains to bind you hand and foot, it usually means they need to keep you alive for some other nefarious purpose. Since you don't know how much time you have, it behooves you to free yourself from your bonds before they enact the next stage of their plan. Since they won't expect you to do this, you may be able to use the element of surprise and turn the tables against them. As long as you're conscious and still breathing when they tie you up, you'll be able to sabotage your bonds so they are more likely to give way later. The trick is to get started the second someone whips out the rope.

1. ACT INDIGNANT.

Your captors will expect you to be angry, so they won't be surprised to see you jut out your jaw, puff up your chest, and tense your muscles as you hurl epithets at them. Good. Pour it on. The most important part of evading rope bonds is to expand and tense your muscles as much as possible while you are being tied up. This may be tough to do throughout your body, all at once, so focus on expanding the area that is being tied first. If they're tying your torso and wrists, fill your lungs with air and take baby breaths. Flex your biceps and forearms. Then, when they switch to your legs, focus on doing the same there. The more you puff up, the larger the loops they'll have to use to bind you.

2. SNEAK SOME WIGGLE ROOM.

If you're badmouthing them as they tie you, they may be too defensive to notice that you are keeping your wrists and ankles slightly apart—about a millimeter or so—while they coil the rope and tie the knots. Whatever you do, don't allow these critical parts of your body to touch each other. Even just a smidgen of air between them will feel like the Grand Canyon later.

3. RELAX.

As soon as they leave you alone, expel all the air from your lungs and relax all your muscles. Now inspect the ropes. If you've done your job, the ropes should be looser now that your muscles are relaxed. Try to determine the integrity of the ropes, the knots, and the object to which they have tied you. Not to disparage the world's ruffians, but most skimp on the rope budget. They use whatever's lying around the castle, and that will tend to be old, possibly fraying, and poorly sized for restraining a human frame. Furthermore, most people do not know how to tie knots properly. This should be obvious upon inspection. In general, the thicker the rope, the harder it is to knot. Thin rope is easier to knot, but it takes less time to cut when abraded against the right surface.

4. PICK AN APPROACH AND WORK QUICKLY.

You don't know how long you've got, so you must work quickly. Decide which classic method of getting free you will use and get cracking.

- **Wriggle:** You might have just enough wiggle room to work free a wrist. Go for it. Don't waste time getting your feet or torso free, since nine times out of ten you'll need to get your hands loose first. Exception: If you need your torso free to lower your mouth to your wrists, do what you gotta do.
- **Abrade or cut:** If you can locate a fixed surface in the room, you can saw through your bonds by rubbing them back and forth against the surface. Ideally, you want a flat, metallic, knifelike surface or a rough texture such as the corner of a brick-and-mortar wall.
- **Manipulate the knots:** Untie the knots by whatever means necessary. Teeth, as noted. Fingers. Or someone else's teeth and fingers.
- **Burn:** Use this method with caution. Remember that when Indy and his father were tied to a pair of chairs, the elder Jones tried to burn the ropes and ended up torching the place. Still, burning is a viable method if you can control the flame or your proximity to it. If you're going to be in the adventure business, avoid wearing thick, flammable tweeds.

ESCAPE CLAUSES

Here are other classic binding scenarios—and corresponding escape options.

- **If you're tied to a chair:** Many chairs are poorly constructed. You may be able to smash it if you propel yourself into a wall using your legs. Or, using your feet, push or pull yourself and the chair close to another object that you can use to abrade your bonds.

- **If your hands are behind you:** Bring your knees up to your chest and work your wrists over your backside, under your legs and feet, and finally over the top of your knees. Once you've successfully gotten your hands in front of you, use your teeth to untie the knots.

- **If you're tied to someone else:** One of you can untie the other, and then vice versa. Often, captors lazily bind two victims together by throwing a loop or two of rope around both captives' torsos. If you both wriggle, one of you may be able to slip under the largest loop and create slack for both of you.

- **If you're tied in a standing position with your arms above your head:** This is an extremely difficult position to work free from, because your legs cannot be used as leverage without causing your weight to drop, further tightening the rope. From the moment you are tied, try not to sag against the restraints. Stand as tall as possible. Wriggle a wrist free, if possible. If you can get your teeth to the knot at your wrists, try manipulation. If you are athletic, damn the torpedoes. Pull yourself up, either using your arms or swinging your legs up to the point where the knot is fastened to a stationary object.

- **If you're bound with duct tape:** This sticky, diabolical restraint was not invented until 1942 and was originally intended for military use. Don't waste your time trying to chew through it; it's too tough. Focus on getting yourself to a sharp surface, which you can use to slice it.

Fig. A

Fig. B

Fig. C

Fig. D

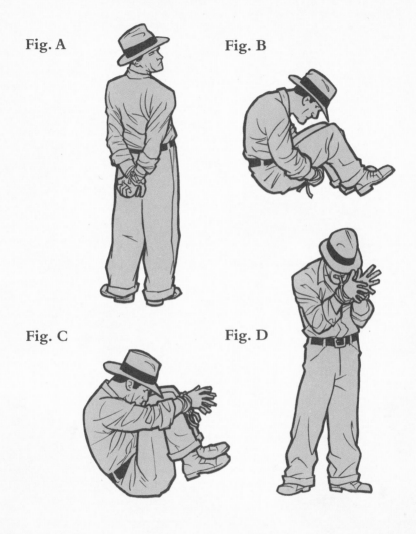

IF YOUR HANDS ARE TIED BEHIND YOU (A), BRING YOUR KNEES TO YOUR CHEST AND WORK YOUR HANDS UNDER YOUR BOTTOM (B) AND OVER THE TOPS OF YOUR KNEES (C). THEN WORK THE KNOTS WITH YOUR TEETH (D).

CHAPTER 4

THE ANIMAL KINGDOM

During archaeological expeditions, so much attention is paid to the artifacts sought and the rivals you seek to best in finding them that it is easy to overlook the other creatures that might get involved. From flying mammals to crawling insects, members of every level of the animal kingdom will surround you—whether you like it or not.

Many of them will also be a necessary part of your journey. Much of the terrain you will cover may not be suited to automobiles, let alone have roads of any kind, so animals will likely be used to transport you, your supplies, or both. However, not all of your encounters with the animal kingdom will be pleasant. There are some deadly creatures lurking on land, in water, and in the sky, and you need to be prepared for as many circumstances as possible.

HOW TO MOUNT AND RIDE A HORSE

Archaeological excavations of chariot burials—where chariot, horse, and driver are buried together—indicate that horses have been domesticated for thousands of years. And for good reason; a horse can be a worthy ally and companion on many different kinds of expeditions. True, the animal cannot travel as fast as a car or a truck, but it does have several advantages over man-made vehicles. For starters, horses require no fuel other than simple food and water. An opponent's vehicle may run out of gas, but your horse will not.

More importantly, a horse can maneuver tight spots and go places other vehicles cannot. For this reason, an element of surprise can be achieved while on horseback. Riding along a ridge parallel to a road, for example, can give you an excellent advantage when you're hoping to catch others off-guard. Indy used this tactic with great success when pursuing Belloq and the Germans' convoy after his escape from the Well of Souls.

And, horses have excellent vision under a variety of conditions. Your mode of transportation might see something you don't—a poisonous snake, for example—and save your neck in the process. To take full advantage of a horse's potential, it helps to understand a few basic pointers.

MOUNTING THE HORSE

For our purposes, we will assume that you are mounting the horse from a standing position and not trying to leap onto the animal from, say, a moving vehicle. If your horse is not equipped with a saddle and stirrups, skip ahead to the next paragraph. Otherwise, you can follow these basic instructions:

1. Standing to the left of the horse, grab the reins and mane in your left hand.
2. Place your left foot in the stirrups, toes forward (not toward the horse).
3. Hold the pommel—or front of the saddle—with your right hand.
4. Push off the ground with your right foot, then shift your body weight to the left foot.
5. Swing your right leg over the horse.
6. Place your right foot in the stirrup and take the reins.

If there is no saddle, you'll be riding bareback. Mounting the horse will require a little more effort on your part. Depending on the size of the horse—and your own size, as well—you may need to find something to stand on in order to mount effectively.

1. Standing to the left of the horse, grab the mane.
2. Jump up and use the mane to pull yourself onto the horse's back.
3. Slide on your stomach, if you must, until you are able to swing your leg over the far side of the animal.

STARTING, STOPPING, AND TURNING

Most horses—except for the stubborn ones—do not need too much encouragement to begin walking. Simply squeeze the horse with your lower legs and increase pressure if the horse doesn't respond. In the case of a quick get-

GRAB THE POMMEL AND STEP INTO THE STIRRUPS.

SWING LEG OVER HORSE. INSERT FOOT INTO STIRRUPS, AND GRAB REINS.

away, however, you may need to move faster. Increase the pressure with your legs, lean forward, and intermittently tap the horse's body with your heels. This will give the horse the signal to pick up the pace. To stop, pull back gently on the reins. If the horse doesn't slow down at all, pull a little harder. Once the horse begins to respond, you can stop pulling. Do not yank on the reins.

The same technique is used to turn left or right. We will use left as an example here: Pull back slightly on the left side of the reins, while putting added pressure on the left side of the horse's body with your left leg. Once the horse responds, you can to relax.

HOW TO MOUNT AND RIDE AN ELEPHANT

Humans have interacted with elephants since ancient times. Based on stone artifacts found in the Indus Valley—in modern Pakistan and northeast India—we can speculate that the people who lived there may have domesticated the elephant as far back as 2,300 BCE. These huge creatures were used mostly for travel and farm work, but also in war. The Carthaginian general Hannibal rode elephants over the Alps to battle the Romans about 200 BCE. And some scholars argue that the discovery of an elephant skull may have sparked the Cyclops myth. (The giant nasal passage may have looked like an eye socket.)

Elephants are still revered in India. The Hindu god Ganesha, as you know, is depicted with the head of an elephant, a symbol of scholarly wisdom. The elephant's trunk embodies "Om"—the eternal sound of the universe. As a result, in India one does not simply hop on an elephant and ride it as one would a horse. The two creatures are not alike in their temperaments and docility, as songstress Willie Scott discovered when she kicked up a fuss about her animal's smell and was shrugged off into a mud pool. Keep her mistake in mind if you need to book an elephant, and remember the following tips.

1. LISTEN TO YOUR MAHOUT.

Elephants are raised from birth or wild-capture by mahouts, who give their lives to this profession. Some mahouts work exclusively with a particular animal from birth to death. The mahout will coach you on how to mount and dismount the animal, and those specific instructions should supersede the general ones given here. All animals are different, and you don't want to make a mistake with Earth's largest land creature.

2. REMOVE YOUR SHOES.

It is said that one rides an elephant barefoot to show respect for the deity, but going shoeless is practical as well; it allows you to tread more gently upon the elephant's skin and grip it with your toes. In some regions, you may be able to get away with wearing soft slippers or lighter footwear, but always investigate before you attempt to mount the animal.

3. KNOW YOUR TECHNIQUE.

Depending upon how the elephant has been trained, you will mount by one of two ways. In the foot-to-neck maneuver, the mahout will instruct the elephant to raise its right foot. Place your own right foot onto the elephant's, and pull yourself up by grabbing hold of its right ear. Do so gently. You want to end up at the top of the animal's back, lying flat on your stomach, which feels soft to the animal. When you have regained your composure, sit up and throw your left leg over the animal's back and slide forward until you are sitting atop the elephant's neck, just behind the head. (The slide is always nerve-racking, so be prepared.) The other method is a little trickier: Face the elephant, step on its trunk, and climb its trunk and forehead, using the ears for a grip, until you reach your seat at the neck. Doing this successfully will require some practice. If the animal is fitted with a howdah (a ceremonial seat), it may kneel and you'll clamber up, but this method is reserved for dignitaries . . . and wusses.

4. RIDE, RIDE, RIDE.

It's unlikely that you will be allowed to take the elephant out for a spin unattended. You will probably always be in the company of the mahout, who directs the elephant using a series of voice commands and gentle prods from a hooked stick. If you are willing and can communicate well with the mahout, he may teach you a few commands and let you trot around the camp to practice. But if all you need is to get from point A to point B, don't waste time. Focus on your expedition, your goals, and your artifacts and let the man drive the elephant. That's what you're paying him for.

USE ELEPHANT'S FOOT AS A STEP.
PULL YOURSELF UP BY THE EAR.

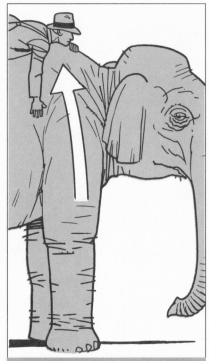

HUG YOUR WAY TO THE TOP OF THE
ANIMAL.

SIT UP AND SLIDE FORWARD TO THE ELEPHANT'S NECK.

5. BEWARE OF SCAMS.

The common practice is to determine a fee and pay for your ride before mounting the elephant. But some unscrupulous mahouts may refuse to let you off the elephant unless you pay a second fee. If that happens, appeal to his conscience by telling him that such behavior is disrespectful to the animal. (Don't worry, he'll get the deity reference.) If that doesn't work, and you haven't regularly trained to leap ten feet without hurting yourself, by all means agree to pay and get off the damned thing.

6. DISMOUNT WHEN THE ELEPHANT STOPS MOVING.

Most likely, the animal will slowly drop its rump to the ground and fold its front legs under itself. Pull your left leg up and over its neck, and slide down to the ground. Pay the mahout and get out of there. Sure, you can try reneging on your promise, but remember: In some cultures, elephants were used as executioners who squashed the heads of the condemned. You don't want to find out if Jumbo has that little number in his bag of tricks.

GIANT VAMPIRE BATS

Not all bats feed on blood. In fact, only three of the 1,100 species of bats in the world do. Vampire bats are so named because, yes, they do feed on blood. Contrary to the popular belief that they latch on to a victim's neck and start drinking like Dracula, all the little suckers really do is bite and then lap up the blood that oozes from the wound. The anticoagulant in their saliva helps keep things running smoothly. Vampire bats are normally quite small; some are not much larger than the average thumb. Giant vampire bats, on the other hand, are said to have wing spans the size of predatory birds. Though long believed by many scientists to be extinct, there are some cryptozoologists who believe in their continued existence and claim to have spotted them, sometimes traveling in large colonies. Indiana Jones is one such scientist, having seen the flying mammals while en route to Pankot Palace in India to recover the Sankara Stones. Though the creatures may be seen during the day, they generally eat at night, so be extra alert if traveling after dark.

HOW TO HANDLE TARANTULAS

Few insects have the notoriety of the tarantula. Sprawling, hairy, and poisonous, the family Theraphosidae proudly boasts among their ranks some of the largest spiders on the planet. The aptly named Goliath tarantula of South America can achieve a leg span of one foot. Tarantulas are found throughout the world, but they are most common in arid, tropical, and subtropical regions. Chances are, you will run into one at some point in your career. But they're not all dangerous—some people even keep them at home and train them as pets. These tips should help make the encounter a relatively uneventful one.

1. KNOW WHAT YOU'RE LOOKING FOR.

There are a number of species of tarantulas of varying sizes and colors: red, brown, black, blue, striped . . . the fuzzy creatures come in many different guises. Familiarize yourself with the most common species of tarantula—and other dangerous insects, for that matter—found at your destination. Many tarantulas live in burrows in the ground, whereas others make their homes in trees or logs.

2. KNOW THEIR HABITS.

Tarantulas are (thankfully) not the most active of spiders. They like to lounge about in their burrows, saving up their energy for hunting prey (they don't have the luxury of a web) and performing mating dances. However, they do tend to be more on the move in the late afternoon and evening, so keep a particular eye out during these times of day. If you happen to be traveling in the fall, take heed. That's when tarantulas mate, and there is nothing like a little sexual tension to put an already predatory species on edge. If you're lucky, the worse you'll encounter is a "guys' night out" of male tarantulas. As soon as you add a female to the mix, these spiders get rather jumpy.

3. WATCH YOUR HANDS.

The hairs on tarantulas are one of their main defense systems and can cause reactions ranging from itching to inflammation if the little buggers rub their legs together, press their plump tummies into your skin, or otherwise inject you with their barbed tresses. Be careful if you have used your bare hands to brush tarantulas off yourself or someone else and keep your hands

USE YOUR BULLWHIP TO BRUSH AWAY PESKY TARANTULAS.

away from your eyes. Eye inflammation can bring a premature end to your expedition. If you do get some "urticating" hairs, as they're called, on your skin, you can remove them with tape. Or you can avoid the entire situation by brushing off tarantulas with your bullwhip, the preferred technique of Indiana Jones.

IF YOU ARE BITTEN

Seek immediate medical treatment. Tarantula bites are not fatal, but some species pack a more potent punch than others. If professional on-site medical help is not available, proceed with the following:

- Treat the bite with an antiseptic if you have one. If not, use soap and water. Bandage quickly.
- Keep an eye on the bite site. Swelling for up to 6 hours is not unusual. However, if after 12 hours you still notice swelling, you need medical assistance.
- As with other reactions, the symptoms may be treated with antihistamines. However, if the reactions include dizziness or swelling around the face and eyes, or if breathing becomes difficult or restricted, it may be necessary to administer epinephrine (an injectable form of adrenaline).
- Stay aware. One of the greatest risks involved with a tarantula bite is the possibility of infection. Fever, muscle spasms, continued difficulty breathing or swallowing, vomiting, diarrhea, or any other alarming effects may be a sign of conditions ranging from septicemia to tetanus; seek medical treatment if you experience any of these symptoms.
- If you are in the southern Italian town of Taranto, where the tarantula was given its name, you may be encouraged to dance a lively

tarantella to stave off death. There is no scientific reason to do this, but it is advisable to go ahead and kick up your heels in order to blend in, meet some locals, and, who knows, maybe even sweat out some venom.

CROCODILES

These fierce water dwellers feed primarily on other reptiles, fish, and mammals—a menu that, unfortunately, includes the human species. Crocodiles are very fast on land and in water, and they often quietly wait for the right tasty treat to come along. The larger species of crocodile can be aggressive and extremely dangerous to humans. Indy, Willie Scott, and Short Round almost found out just how dangerous crocodiles can be when Dr. Jones severed the rope bridge on which they were standing, sending many of Mola Ram's men—and eventually Mola Ram himself—into the gaping mouths of the crocs below. Here's the bright side: Although their bite is known to pack up to 3,000 pounds of pressure per square inch, once that jaw is closed, it is very difficult for them to open it again. So, if you ever have the unfortunate luck to be in close proximity with a crocodile, keep in mind that their heads cannot move extensively from side to side, so try to stay to the periphery. Watch out for their claws, though, which can do serious damage. And, if you can manage to do so, clamp or tie their snouts shut.

HOW TO HANDLE POISONOUS SNAKES

When the Egyptian Queen Cleopatra committed suicide by allowing herself to be bitten by an asp—more specifically, an Egyptian cobra—she was letting herself be killed by an animal of great symbolic power, one that is found on the headpieces of the pharaohs. From the wreath of snakes around the Hindu god Siva's neck to the snake crawling up the caduceus, snakes have inspired and terrorized humans for thousands of years, representing everything from omniscience to temptation.

That said, they don't have many fans. Indiana Jones's dislike of the slithery creatures—also known as *ophidiophobia*—is well documented and, according to his memoirs, dates to his youth, when he tumbled into a tank full of snakes while being chased by looters on a train traveling through Utah. As luck would have it, he encountered thousands of the reptiles—including the king cobra—while interred against his will in the Well of Souls in Tanis, Egypt, with Marion Ravenwood.

Snakes are found in virtually every corner of the world, and if fieldwork is going to be a major part of your career, snakes are very likely to cross your path at some point. Many of the tombs and tunnels we explore have been purposely seeded with snakes to protect the precious, and sometimes revered, contents from vandals and looters. This works more often than not. Just the same, ophidiophobe or not, you have to be able to maintain your calm around these creatures. Here are some pointers.

1. KNOW THE LOCALS.

Many snakes—most, really—are harmless. Of course, some of the more deadly species are so-called because they are quite aggressive. It is in your best interest to know what the primary species are in the region to which you will be traveling and how to identify them. When excavating in Egypt, for example, you can expect to hear a lot about venomous asps, another name for the Egyptian cobra. In India, you may encounter the king cobra, the largest venomous snake in the world.

2. BE AWARE OF YOUR SURROUNDINGS.

Some snakes like to live in trees, whereas others prefer holes in the ground, swamps, or a warm, toasty rock. When walking through the grass, beat the bushes with a walking stick or staff to alert snakes to your presence. Take particular care when lifting rocks, and always wear protective gloves before thrusting your hands into a dark, closed, or otherwise obscured orifice.

3. KEEP YOUR DISTANCE.

One of the techniques that snake charmers use—and that you, too, can employ—is to stay out of striking range. In the case of a cobra, that is roughly one-third of the snake's length. In the case of a fifteen-foot king cobra, however, that's at least five feet.

4. WATCH YOUR EYES.

Snakebite is not the only thing to fear. Even if you can put some distance between yourself and the snake, some cobras can spray their venom farther

A TRAUMATIC ENCOUNTER WITH SNAKES MAY RESULT IN LIFELONG OPHIDIOPHOBIA.

than their striking range. It will temporarily blind you if it comes in contact with your eyes, which makes it rather difficult to continue defending yourself. For protection tips, review the suggestions for standard gear on pages 18–23.

5. DRESS FOR THE OCCASION.

Although she never could have anticipated being sealed inside the snake-ridden Well of Souls, Marion Ravenwood's ensemble is a perfect example of what not to wear to a snake fest. Open-toed shoes or sneakers are obviously not a good idea on an expedition, no matter how high the mercury rises. Boots that cover your ankles and have steel-reinforced toes are ideal.

6. MOVE SLOWLY.

Most snakes do not want to come in contact with humans. We're sure you feel the same way. In close quarters, however, it is best not to make any sudden movements that may appear threatening, especially if an aggressive snake, such as a king cobra, is upright and its hood is spread. Do as Indy did: Simply back away slowly until you have reached a safe distance.

7. FIRE IT UP.

If you're stuck in a pit full of snakes, it's no time for modesty. Fashion a torch from anything available—and that includes clothing, bones, etc. If you have ignored the previous advice to dress appropriately, a little lace number like the one Belloq gave to Marion fans a fine flame. Waving a torch or other flame-bearing device at snakes can sometimes help keep them at bay; other times it just makes them really mad. Also keep in mind that under cold weather conditions it can backfire, and the snakes may actually be drawn to the heat source. If the snakes are a definite threat, your only option may be to douse them with a petrochemical and ignite them. Do so under only the most extreme circumstances, and keep in mind that the burning reptiles may flee in your direction—and they won't be happy.

IF YOU'RE BITTEN

Some snakes have highly toxic venom but are very skittish and unlikely to come in contact with humans. Others may be less venomous by comparison but are much more likely to attack, delivering large quantities of venom in a single bite. Although the cobra's venom is certainly not the deadliest, it is capable of delivering high volumes of venom in a single bite. One bite can be enough to kill an elephant.

Many snake venoms contain neurotoxins and/or hemotoxins that attack both the nervous system and the body's tissues. In short, you need to get medical attention as soon as possible. If you are entombed against your will, it will be difficult to head to the nearest emergency room, so proceed as follows:

- Wash the area with soap and water.
- Do your best to keep the area immobile. It may be advisable to devise a splint for the bitten area.
- To keep the venom from spreading, wrap the area several inches above the bite to slow the spread, but DO NOT cut off circulation or apply a tourniquet.
- DO NOT apply ice.
- You can make attempts to remove the venom. However, the suck-

and-spit method is rarely effective, and it might endanger the individual doing the sucking and spitting. It also increases the possibility of infection, since the mouth houses a potpourri of bacteria. If someone in your group has a first-aid kit with a syringe that has a suction attachment, use it. Some apothecaries in rural areas also sell small, simple suction devices that you can carry in your rucksack. Again, these devices and various venom-removal techniques have mixed results. Your time would be better spent finding a medical facility that can administer antivenom.

Remember, snake meat is eaten in various corners of the world, so if you do manage to corral a snake, you may want to make a meal out of it. Cook it first, though, since eating raw snake meat may lead to parasitic infections with potentially fatal complications. After all, if you've survived an encounter with a live snake, why risk being harmed by a dead one?

HOW TO DEAL WITH RATS

In Hindu statuary, the god Ganesha is often depicted riding on the back of a well-dressed rat. Indians do not revere rats especially, but they do know that rats are the superheroes of the rodent world. They'll gnaw through wood, plastic, glass, asbestos, mortar, and concrete in search of the single ounce of food they must consume each day to stay alive. They will burrow under and into your home to swipe unattended snacks. They'll roost in your fruit trees; plunder your garden; nest in your attic and walls; scavenge through your garbage; swim up your sewer line and crawl out your toilet. Their physical abilities make them far more destructive and dangerous than their smaller cousins. And while those cuddly mice scurry at our footfall, rats are more likely to attack unprovoked.

Clearly, the symbolism in these ancient artifacts suggests that Ganesha, imbued with the powers of his rat companion, was capable of all things. Chinese lore also celebrates rats for their cleverness, ingenuity, ability to amass things of great value, and unmatched survival instincts. But Westerners do not look at rats so charitably. Perhaps we are still reminded of the medieval Black Death, which wiped out a third of Europe's population in an orgy of blood and pus. Not for a moment did the great minds of medieval Europe suspect that the flea that brought the plague rode into their midst on the back of the common rat. Only later did scientists piece the puzzle together, and since then we have given rats a wide berth.

It is unlikely that you will encounter rats when excavating a "dry" site. If rats are present, there must be a source of food and water. Unfortunately, what they're eating doesn't necessarily meet our criteria for food. When Indiana Jones and Nazi go-to gal Elsa Schneider entered the catacombs of Venice, they stumbled upon thousands of rats that had apparently been feasting upon an unholy mélange of urban sewage and mummified flesh. Their simple approach was to sidestep the critters, but you may need to take stronger measures.

1. DRESS FOR THE WORST.

If you suspect you will encounter a large number of rats, wear tall leather boots, preferably ones that close with Velcro or covered snaps. Tuck in your pants and cover your shoelaces. If you give them any sort of toehold, they will clamber up your body and get under your clothing.

2. WATCH FOR THEIR TRAIL.

Rats are nocturnal, so they may not be around when you are working. If your site has been disturbed but there are no rodents visible, look for droppings that range from 1/2 inch to 3/4 inch in length, and gnaw holes about two inches (5 cm) or larger. Look for black streaks along walls, objects, and openings from the outside. Their greasy fur picks up dirt and wipes it on whatever surfaces it touches. Sniff the air for the unmistakable scent of urine. Check for the absence of any camp food, the presence of fur sheddings, and nearby burrows.

DAMP, DARK CAVERNS ARE A PARADISE FOR RODENTIA.

3. IF YOU SEE RATS, TRY TO DISTRACT OR SHOO THEM.

Usually, rodents will scatter when you appear and make some noise, but you cannot count on that. Rats are bold and unpredictable. If you wish to distract them, toss a bit of food in a direction opposite from where you need to pass. But remember, because of their poor eyesight, it may take a while for them to identify the food source.

4. IF ALL ELSE FAILS, TAKE THEM OUT.

If you have no food or they don't take your bait, immolation may be the only way to clear the area, though this task is admittedly unsavory and gruesome. If only a few rats threaten you, use your bullwhip. A single, well-directed flick will disable or kill a rodent. If all else fails, it is not unheard of to take out a savvy campsite rat with a sharpshooter. Watch for the glint of their eyes before firing.

IF YOU ARE BITTEN

The bite of a rat has been likened to the cut of a razor. They can spread their bottom incisors to get a better grip and deliver a nastier bite. A rat's bite is more powerful than a crocodile's, and it packs 7,000 pounds of pressure per square inch. It would be wrong to say that all rats are diseased, but many carry dangerous pathogens. If you haven't had a tetanus vaccination in more than ten years, you're at greater risk. So get that shot before leaving for your expedition—and if you get a bite, follow these tips.

1. Clean the wound after letting it bleed a bit. Use soapy water, if possible.

2. Poke the wound quickly with burning embers from a piece of wood; this will cauterize it. Then splash alcohol onto the wound to clean it. Do not put anything flammable on the wound after the alcohol—unless you're seeking third-degree burns as well.

3. Head to a hospital as soon as possible. If you have killed a rat, bring its carcass to the hospital to test for rabies.

4. In addition to rabies, wild rats may carry *Spirillum minus* and *Streptobacillus moniliformis*, which cause rat-bite fever, so antibiotics are a must. Doxycycline comes in handy; ask your doctor for a prescription before you leave home.

5. Take echinacea elixir or lomatium elixir and lots of vitamin C to boost the immune system. (These should all be items in your field kit.) Native American medicine men carry herbs for this kind of emergency, so a nearby reservation may come in handy.

MONKEYS

They're cute and entertaining. You can dress them up, place smart hats on their furry little heads, and carry them around like living, breathing, baby dolls. You can teach monkeys to do anything from grind an organ box to salute. But in the end, you can't trust them. These clever, highly trainable creatures can also be devious and treacherous, often acting as scouts or decoys. Don't be deceived by the wide eyes and clingy affection. They do, however, make excellent food tasters. If you ever have any questionable dates in the house, feed them to the monkey first.

INSECTS

INSECTS

Nothing reveals the gaps in human knowledge as much as the class Insecta. There are one million named species of bugs in the world, but scientists estimate there are nine million more that haven't even been classified. Other scientists scoff, saying the true number of unknown species is closer to—hold onto your hat—fifty million. Chances are great that you will encounter a hideous insect you have never seen in a textbook. Give it wide berth. Evolutionarily speaking, insects are plentiful because they are so expendable. But that doesn't mean they don't have a nasty defense mechanism that pierces human flesh.

As Indy knows all too well, four-inch ants or giant mosquitoes possess huge pincers or proboscides. If you are entering dark, damp, icky places, wear sturdy boots, a thick hat, long-sleeved shirts, and long pants. Thick leather gloves are also advisable, though you should never handle an insect you cannot identify. While searching for the Chachapoyan fertility idol, Indy swept away tarantulas (technically arachnids) on his guide Satipo's back with his coiled bullwhip. In India, Willie Scott stepped gingerly among the creepy-crawlies on her way to rescue Short Round and Indy from the spiked cavern. Sure, if you aspire to a PhD in entomology in addition to one in archaeology, corral insects in a collecting jar for further study. Otherwise, stand back and let the beasties go their merry way. Their time on earth is short, and they spend much of it scavenging for food. But it doesn't have to be you.

CHAPTER 5

ON-SITE SKILLS

Although there is no substitute for a fine education and extensive research, most of what makes you an exceptional archaeologist is what you learn in the field. No matter how well you prepare or how many contingency plans you have, you are bound to encounter surprises—not all of them pleasant. That said, being well prepared will allow you to get the most out of your on-site experiences and—ideally—ensure that you make it home in one piece.

WHEN PLANNING AN EXCAVATION, BE PREPARED TO WORK AROUND THE CLOCK.

HOW TO LOCATE A LOST
ARCHAEOLOGICAL SITE

Archaeology exists because long-dead humans and the winds of time are clever at hiding things from sight. To excel in your work, you must develop a knack for uncovering the hidden. There are only a handful of ways to pull this off: research, oral history, and personal observation.

1. HIT THE BOOKS.

There's a lot to be said for spending your Friday nights in the library. Books are the repository of humankind's wisdom, and the better the library, the more sources you'll have at your disposal. Your best leads will come from primary sources—original ancient texts—because you'll glean knowledge directly from the lion's mouth, so to speak, without interpretation by another scholar who is lazy, has an axe to grind, or has a hazy knowledge of Greek. Keep all your findings on a particular subject in one place, and refer to them often. Modern-day knowledge workers use moleskin notebooks, which are neatly bound and have elastic straps—not unlike the diary used by Dr. Henry Jones Sr. to assemble what he learned about the Holy Grail. It pays to write clues exactly as they have been phrased in the original text, because ancient writers deliberately cloaked their meaning with clever wordplay. "Only the penitent man shall pass" is a diabolically subtle way of saying "Kneel." Had the elder Jones copied that line down incorrectly, or paraphrased it, Junior's body would be missing its head. When you transfer your notes to a computer file, always keep your original notebook in case you have incorrectly transcribed something.

2. WORK FROM MAPS.

Indy is fond of saying that "X" never, ever marks the spot, but even he would agree that humans always leave some kind of trail to their most prized possessions. We're not supposed to write down computer passwords, either, but how many of us have ignored that advice? If you are lucky enough to acquire a map to your destination, study it closely for notes, sketches, or other symbols in the margins. Think low-tech: Your predecessors may have used invisible ink or coded pinpricks to remind themselves or to pass along an important caveat to a treasure-seeker following in their footsteps.

3. VISIT A MAP ROOM.

The map room at Tanis looked unique, but sites that use astronomical markers are not uncommon. Stonehenge itself was designed to impart information with the help of the sun. You'll need to assemble some props if you encounter a map room on your travels. Typically, you'll need to identify an opening to the outdoors for a light source, be it solar or lunar. You'll need a pointing device, which in Indy's case was the Staff of Ra. And you'll need a reference point; Indy's was the hole in which he inserted the staff. Be warned: Gathering all three of these items won't be easy. The Staff of Ra, for example, consisted of two pieces. Without one, the other was useless. As for reference points, the ancients were fond of the four main ones found in the astronomical/celestial year: the vernal equinox, the summer solstice, the autumnal equinox, and the winter solstice. Finally, if you manage to locate the headpiece of a staff-like pointer, do yourself a favor and study both sides.

4. LOOK FOR EMBEDDED SYMBOLS.

It took Indy no time at all to pinpoint the location of the dead knight's tomb in a Venetian library, because he knew symbols could be every-where—on statues, floor tiles, even stained glass windows. To work quickly, you must be open to what your environment is telling you, and you must realize that you are not always standing in the right place. Don't abandon your search until you have changed your perspective a couple of times. You don't know where the person who hid the item was standing, how clever he or she was, or how nuts.

5. IF THE LOCALS ARE TALKING, PAY ATTENTION.

Academics always give the locals short shrift, but sometimes it pays to put down the books and listen to what people are saying about the object of your quest. Yes, interpreting folklore can be like a multigenerational game of telephone, but occasionally some fertile seed can be separated from the chaff. Obviously, the Brotherhood of the Cruciform Sword knew the loca-tion of the Holy Grail; this knowledge is so crucial that it passed down through the generations intact and correct. Good luck getting those boys to talk, however.

WHEN USING ANCIENT HEADPIECES, BE SURE TO READ THE SMALL PRINT—ON BOTH SIDES.

HOW TO EXCAVATE A SITE

The classic way of "knocking down" an archaeological site is to proceed at a glacier's pace. First, you survey the site, looking for clues to what lies beneath the surface, occasionally digging small holes to characterize, or "describe" the site. When you have developed a plan of attack, you use a fixed point in the region to map the site in the shape of a grid pattern. Waterproof string and sturdy stakes are used to build the physical grid. Slowly, you and your able-bodied assistants excavate the earth in one-meter-square blocks, peeling back the dirt one millimeter at a time using brushes and other delicate tools. Copious notes are taken, and changes in the soil color are cause for excitement (it indicates a transition zone for the site). All soil is sifted through screens in search of minuscule artifacts—broken crockery, dried seed husks, ancient coals—that will eventually be milked ad nauseum for someone's PhD thesis. All items are assigned a catalog number that is linked to each grid block. You keep such painstaking records because with each swish of the brush, each pick of the tool, you are destroying the site. In the end, the soil will be gone, but your written record will remain.

That's how archaeology is normally done—but sometimes we have hostile madmen on our trails. If you don't have the time to conduct a leisurely, academic analysis of a site, don't. Forget about what your fustier colleagues would say and switch to a grab-and-go style of archaeology. If the bad guys get to the artifact first, it will disappear into some despot's collection forever. If you nab it, it'll end up in a museum.

1. ARRANGE YOUR TRANSPORTATION FIRST.

It helps to work backward. Assuming time is of the essence, you should know where you're going with your artifact once you pull it out of its lair. If you need a tramp steamer, make sure there's one in port and you have the captain's cell phone number. If you're flying out, make sure the pontoon pilot knows to leave his pet python at home. If the object is large or fragile and needs to be protected during transport, make sure you have your packing materials and excelsior. Be sure your papers are in order in case you are stopped at border crossings. This way, if you have to split in a hurry, you've nailed down your exit strategy.

2. ASSEMBLE TOOLS AND DIGGERS.

Whether you're hiring a group of mercenaries or digging by yourself with the help of a few trusted colleagues, they will probably expect you to bring the tools, water, and couscous—or, at the very least, pay for them. If you're working illicitly on someone else's site, take precautions to avoid detection. It pays to work incognito. During the dig at Tanis, Indy and Sallah suited up in thobes and gutras to blend into the army of local workmen. Their only mistake: Doing nothing to camouflage their site. The lesson: If you can't blend, hide.

RESEARCH A SITE BEFORE VISITING SO YOU CAN BRING THE PROPER TOOLS.

3. STUDY THE SITE.

If you're working alone and have to enter a dangerous place, be sure you've boned up on the research enough to know what you're getting yourself into. When Indy walked into that Chachapoyan temple in the jungles of Peru, he had an idea what was waiting for him, down to the booby-trapped flooring and the idol's counterweighted pedestal. And he had prepared at least one prop—a sandbag—to deal with one of those challenges. In the Well of Souls, he and Sallah knew enough to bring stout poles to lift the Ark of the Covenant from its resting place. It always pays to know how you're going to carry the thing out of there. Arks and rucksacks don't mix.

4. LOOK FOR A GREAT SEAL ON THE WAY IN.

Get in, get out. Oh, if only it were that easy. Sometimes the object you seek was never meant to leave its resting spot, and its original owners have rigged up some way of keeping it there, albeit a curse or some kind of mechanical trigger. Recall that only after he found the Grail did Indy learn that it could not pass beyond the seal emblazoned on the floor of the cave's antechamber. Passing over the spot triggered a quake, and the Grail was lost in the earth's crust—along with Dr. Elsa Schneider.

The most famous curse on record is the one inscribed on King Tut's tomb: "The wings of death will strike down he who disturbs the Pharaoh's peace!" Lord Carnarvon, who funded that expedition, died from an infected mosquito bite. He was the first of that expedition to die, but not the last. Modern scientists theorize that bacterial spores in the tombs may have been the cause of Carnarvon's infection. If pathogens are a concern, wear gloves and a face mask, touch nothing but the object you seek, and discard all clothing when you leave.

5. RECORD WHAT YOU KNOW ASAP.

When you've given the bad guys the slip, and you're relaxing with a glass of kir aboard a luxury ocean liner, a zeppelin, or some other stately mode of public transportation, get out your digital recorder or notebook and make careful notes about everything you saw and did at the site. This may be the only chance you have to get the facts straight before the action starts again.

PRESERVING THE INTEGRITY OF SITES AND ARTIFACTS

Archaeological sites belong not to you but to the nations in which they are located. They are the cultural heritage of a specific people and must be respected. So it is your obligation to leave them as intact as possible so future archaeologists can pick up where you left off. You got into this business because you love what the hand of man has wrought, so why travel the world wrecking what you have sworn to protect and cherish? Careful preservation should not be a problem if you have undertaken a laborious, scholarly knock-down of a site, securing all necessary authorizations. But if you've been forced by circumstances to indulge in smash-and-grab archaeology, learn to leave as little damage as possible in your wake.

- Take only what you've come for and leave the rest behind, untouched.

- When digging, be as gentle as possible. Use brushes to work dirt or sand away from an object so you don't break or chip off a piece of an artifact.

- Try to keep the site's opening functional. Whether it's a stone slab or sophisticated mechanical door, make sure it can be shut and continue doing its job until the next visit from the living.

- Refrain from scrawling graffiti. The most fascinating graffiti in the world is the stuff scratched inside the great pyramids by the workmen who built them. Until you've built something that lasts several millennia, you haven't earned the right to scribble your name on a historic monument.

HOW TO IDENTIFY SECRET PASSAGEWAYS AND BOOBY TRAPS

Some people just can't take a hint. Threats carved on entry seals, vicious-looking totems guarding the site, beefy local guides screaming and fleeing . . . sometimes nothing can dissuade an archaeologist on a mission, even if all the signs indicate that she is going to have a hard time getting out with not only the item in question but all her limbs as well. But at least archaeology isn't dull.

So you have your team assembled, and those who haven't already fled in fear of other-worldly tortures are ready to enter. You've already established from signs outside the site itself that you're probably going to encounter some trouble. But you're determined to forge ahead, either because the prize is too great or your sense of mortality is too small. Keep your eyes and ears open.

1. DO YOUR RESEARCH.

There is always a chance that someone has already studied the site you are entering. Ideally, that someone is you, but this is not always the case. Humility is important. Be open to the possibility that someone may know more about it than you do. Use their knowledge. Dr. Henry Jones Sr. made Grail lore his life's work, and it really paid off. The clues he had assembled in his diary saved not only his own life but Indy's as well.

2. WATCH FOR SIGNS ON YOUR WAY IN.

A passageway strewn with bones and decapitated bodies is a not-so-subtle indication that you could be in a danger zone. Let the misfortune of those who have gone before you be your advantage. First, look at how they died. Blow darts in the throat? They had to come from somewhere. Try to determine the angle of entry and from which direction they came. Look at where the poor schmuck was standing. Did he step on or into something? Do your best to learn from their fatal mistakes.

3. DO NOT GO GENTLE INTO THAT GOOD LIGHT.

If you are working your way through a dark tunnel, a ray of light may look like a welcome respite from your grim surroundings. That's just what tribes like the South American Hovitos are counting on. This is not the afterlife—if you're lucky—and you are not trying to cross over. So, stay away from the light unless you want to become a human shish kebab. A spear through a major organ is not covered in emergency first aid.

4. LOOK UP, LOOK DOWN, LOOK ALL AROUND.

Oh, they were clever, those ancients. It's not enough to watch where you're going. You need to look above, behind, and underfoot. Be suspicious of everything. If the room is dry and sandy, yet for some reason there's moss covering the floor stones, it may be covering a trap. When approaching a floor covered in stepping stones, for example, be sure to examine the stones carefully before nonchalantly skipping across them on your way to the altar. Do they all look the same? Do any stand out? Sometimes tossing a weighted item—a rock, a bag of sand—on the ground before crossing can trigger a reaction, and then you'll know what you're about to step into.

5. TUNE IN TO THE ELEMENTS.

In addition to changes in light patterns, be sure to watch for a sudden, swift breeze, faraway noises, or tremors. Should you notice such a drastic change in your elemental surroundings, hit the dirt. Though there's no way to know what's coming, most booby traps are designed to take out a bipedal adult. Cutting your height may cut your risk (and, ideally, leave other things intact).

MANY BOOBY TRAPS FEATURE A (HIDDEN) EMERGENCY RELEASE LEVER.

6. WHEN IN DOUBT, DON'T TOUCH.

When traveling in pairs or groups, walk one behind the other. Standing still works, but remember that any surface can be booby trapped. Short Round learned this lesson the hard way when he leaned against a wall in a secret passageway in Pankot Palace, only to set off a trap that caused spikes to protrude from the floor and the collapsing ceiling. Visible irregularities in walls and floors could be buttons or levers. Beware of furniture, too: Chairs, urns, a fireplace tool set, or other seemingly decorative items may in fact be levers in disguise.

7. LEAVE YOUR MARK.

As you make your way to your interior destination, remember that you're going to have to get back out again. If you've bested some of the traps on the way in, do your darndest to jam them so that they won't get you on the way back out.

8. MOVE CAUTIOUSLY—ESPECIALLY WHEN YOU SPOT THE TREASURE.

The minute you lay eyes on the prize is the same moment in which you must stop, take a breather, and reexamine your next move. If you think the booby traps on the way in were bad, imagine what's in store for you just steps away from the big score. Don't get overanxious.

9. KNOW WHAT TO TAKE AND WHAT TO LEAVE BEHIND.

Items that have been hidden away in temples and guarded by elaborately constructed traps are obviously meant by their original owners to stay exactly where they are. Although they may be better off in a museum, remember that in some cases you just have to leave the party alone. Whenever you are having trouble deciding whether to take something or leave it behind, remember the following: The wrong choice could cost a life, or at least an appendage.

10. FINALLY, REMAIN SKEPTICAL—EVEN AFTER YOU'VE CLAIMED YOUR PRIZE.

Just because something horrible doesn't happen right away doesn't mean it isn't going to happen. Remain vigilant until you and your treasure are on the other side of that threat-laden entry you completely ignored.

WARNING: If you set off a booby trap, there may be a fulcrum release lever, often in the same floor or wall that triggered the trap in the first place. If there are any obvious holes or crevices, take a deep breath, break a few nails, and stick your hand in there to see what you find. You might get lucky.

LOOTERS AND LOOTING

Though things were different in Indy's day, modern archaeologists must register with their host nation, work under the auspices of a local authority such as a museum or cultural agency, and declare all items discovered in their work. Since World War II, a number of important international treaties—such as the 1970 UNESCO Convention on the Means of Prohibiting and Preventing the Illicit Import, Export, and Transfer of Ownership of Cultural Property and the 1995 UNIDROIT Convention on Stolen or Illegally Exported Cultural Objects—have been enacted to protect the cultural heritage of all nations. Unfortunately, not all nations have signed the treaties, and even if they have, the treaties are not retroactive. The 1995 law requires citizens or entities (such as museums) with a known stolen object in their possession to return the object to its rightful nation. This is an ongoing process throughout the world, and several priceless artifacts and artworks stolen by the Nazis are still making their way home after sixty years. Though experts constantly debate the merits and strengths of these laws, you are expected to comply with them fully—or relinquish your hat and bullwhip.

HOW TO DECIPHER HIEROGLYPHS AND LOST LANGUAGES

Making sense of what you see on-site will be largely dependent on your ability to work with multiple languages, even those from before your time. Beyond ancient Greek and Latin—both of which you should know cold—you may encounter any number of languages, from various Hindu dialects to Cuneiform to early Phoenician. Though you may not be able to decipher every symbol or language you see, having a few of the biggies under your belt can make the difference between opening a container that reads, "Here lies Pharaoh Ptolemy V Epiphanes," and one that reads, "DANGER! Do Not Open! Wrath of God Inside."

HIEROGLYPHS

Hieroglyphic writing is one form with which you should become familiar, as your pursuits will undoubtedly take you to Egypt at some point. Thanks to the Rosetta Stone, we are now able to translate hieroglyphics. Discovered by a French soldier under Napoleon's rule, the Rosetta Stone is carved with hieroglyphs, demotic script (a later form of hieroglyphs), and ancient Greek. Eventually, the Greek translation made it possible to decipher the meaning of hieroglyphic writings, and it is said to have taken Frenchman Jean-François Champollion fourteen years to get the job done. The translation of hieroglyphics has completely changed our interaction with Egyptian sites and artifacts.

There are three basic types of ancient Egyptian writing:

- **Hieroglyphic** is the most formal, and therefore heiroglyphs are found on objects of significance such as temples and tombs.
- **Hieratic** is a simpler script form that was used on a daily basis—in business, for example. It foregoes a lot of the elaborate drawings, and it resembles cursive.
- **Demotic** is a later version of the hieroglyphs, more closely resembling hieratic. Though occasionally used for other, more formal purposes, it was generally used administratively.

We will focus on hieroglyphs here. Hieroglyphs fall into several major categories:

- **Logograms, ideograms, and pictograms** are symbols that represent an idea or object.
- **Phonograms** are symbols that represent sounds. A phonogram can represent one, two, or three sounds. And just to make things extra-complicated, a logogram can also be a phonogram. In these cases, a vertical line is added to the symbol to indicate that it should be read as a phonogram instead of a logogram.
- **Determinatives** are essentially "hints" that will help you decipher the meaning of the logograms. We'll talk more about them below.

1. KNOW WHICH WAY IS UP.

Some hieroglyphs were written in horizontal rows; others were written in vertical columns. If written in a column, they should be read from the top down.

2. KNOW WHERE YOU'RE HEADED.

Just to keep things lively, those kooky Egyptians thought to themselves, "Hey, how about we create a written language that's read from left to right some of the time and from right to left the rest of the time? Won't that be a hoot?!" It's true—not all horizontal hieroglyphs should be read in the same direction. But to figure out where to start, just look at the people and animals in the script. They are all facing in the same direction, and that direction represents where you should start reading. For example, if all of the beings are facing the left, that means that you should start at the left and read toward the right. And if you ever see two symbols presented one on top of the other, be aware that the symbol on top is read before the one on the bottom.

3. KNOW YOUR PHONICS.

Hieroglyphic writing is highly phonetic, so you're looking at representations of necessary sounds. English goes a little overboard with the spelling, from the frivolous *ght* to the dreaded silent *e*. Egyptians took the "say more with less" approach.

Plus, they often didn't bother with vowels. In keeping with their simplistic approach, many words omit them. This means a group of consonants might represent more than one word. But the Egyptians fixed that problem by adding what are called determinatives after a symbol or group of symbols to indicate its meaning. Determinatives have no sound; they are just there to give some context to the symbols preceding them and, if necessary, to indicate plurals. The chart on pages 145-147 gives you a breakdown of some basic hieroglyphs.

Ancient Egyptians used these basic hieroglyphs to spell out names, objects, or anything that couldn't be represented by an ideogram (a picture or symbol that represents a person, object, or idea). Hieroglyphs were read phonetically and strung together to form words, like the letters of an alphabet. Each letter was represented by an object, as shown in column 1.

HIEROGLYPHS	SYMBOL	ENGLISH EQUIVALENT	PRONUNCIATION AND USAGE
	vulture	A	_a_board, box_car_, _a_rchaeology
	foot	B	_b_ite, _b_oots, _b_ullwhip
	basket	C	_c_amp, _c_rack, _c_amel Use the folded cloth (s) for the soft _c_ sound. The hilltop (_k_) or the animal stomach (_x_) may be used for hard _ch_ sounds, as in and _ch_ronicle, _ch_asm, and _ch_rome.
	rope	CH	_ch_ase, _ch_ampion, _ch_arge, lur_ch_
	hand	D	_d_iary, _d_ig, mur_d_er, han_d_
	reed leaves	E	d_e_cent, r_ee_d, m_ee_t, stamp_e_de The vulture (a) may be used for _e_ sounds such as _e_lephant, dec_e_nt, and b_e_t.
	horned viper	F	_f_ortress, kni_f_e, _f_edora
	pot stand	G	_g_round, _g_rail, ha_gg_ard The cobra (_j_) may be used for soft _g_ sounds such as _g_eology, _ch_arge, and ar_ch_aeology.

HIEROGLYPHS	SYMBOL	ENGLISH EQUIVALENT	PRONUNCIATION AND USAGE
	rope	H	*hunt*, *behind*, *hat*, *whip* The rope may signify the *wh* sound (when the *w* is largely silent).
	reed leaf	I	*Indiana*, *fight*, *fit* Use the reed leaves for both short and long *i* sounds.
	cobra	J	*jeep*, *jacket* The cobra can also signify soft *g* sounds such as *geology*, *charge*, and *archaeology*.
	hilltop	K	*ark*, *kick*, *key* The hilltop may be used for soft and hard *ch* sounds, as in and *chase*, *chasm*, and *chrome*, as well as for *q*, as in *quail*, *quarter*, and *quicksilver*.
	male lion	L	*lost*, *alligator*, *skull* The *l* sound is nonexistent in ancient Egyptian. When ancient Egyptians wrote foreign words that used this sound, they often used the water (*n*) or the open mouth (*r*) sign.
	owl	M	*map*, *monkey*, *summer*
	water	N	*Nile*, *nuclear*, *tunnel*
	quail chick	O	*blood*, *owl*, *moon* The vulture (*a*) can also be used for hard *o* sounds such as *thought* and *hot*. The quail chick may also be used for *u* sounds such as *queue* and *useful*.
	stool	P	*pyramid*, *supper*, *property* The horned viper may also represent the *ph* sound in words like *pharaoh* and *triumph* (as well as any *f* sound).
	hilltop	Q	*queen*, *liquefy*, *quack* The hilltop (*k*) can represent a *q* sound. Alternatively, combine the basket (*c*) with the quail chick (*o*, *u*, *w*).
	open mouth	R	*roar*, *red*, *error*

HIEROGLYPHS	SYMBOL	ENGLISH EQUIVALENT	PRONUNCIATION AND USAGE
	folded cloth	S	*sea*, *storm*, *curse* The folded cloth may signify the soft *s* sounds for letter *c*, as in *essence*.
	lake	SH	*shell*, *lash*, *marsh* The lake best represents the combined *sh* sound. It may also represent the soft *sch* sound in names like *Schmidt*.
	bread loaf	T	*tiger*, *battle*, *tree* The bread loaf represents *tt* as well as *t*; there is no need to double the loaves, even when they are doubled in English.
	quail chick	U/W	*whip*, *write*, *you* The quail chick should be used for long *u* sounds such as *u* or *oo u*.
	horned viper	V	*vault*, *nerve*, *heavy*, *savvy*
	animal stomach	X	*explode*, *exact*, *hex* Alternatively, combine hilltop (*k*) and the folded cloth (*s*). The animal stomach may also represent the *th* sound in words like *throw* and *width*.
	reed leaves	Y	*Indy*, *carry* Double reed leaves signify the *y* (long *e*) sound. One reed leaf (*i*) can be used to represent the short *i* or *y* sound in words such as *yes*, *young*, and *yellow*.
	door bolt	Z	*zebra*, *puzzle* The door bolt represents both single and double *z* sounds.

Note that vowels didn't exist in ancient Egyptian; think of them as weak consonants. When transcribing an English word using hieroglyphs, ignore vowels except for when they start a word or if a word would be confusing without them (as in a name). For example, *Andrew* may be written as

(ANDRW) and *danger* as

(DANJR).

OTHER LANGUAGES

If you are looking at a language that you are fairly sure is not hieroglyphics, you may wish to employ the assistance of a trained symbologist. Short of that, do your best to use some common sense and logic.

1. LOOK FOR PATTERNS.

Repeated symbols or markings can be clues to meaning. If something shows up a lot, it's probably very important and perhaps a key symbol of the language.

2. THINK LITERALLY.

When dealing with symbols that are pictures of specific things, the meaning is probably rather straightforward. A carving of a tree, for example, might represent (what else?) a tree. As academics, we are trained to constantly seek out a deeper meaning, but when it comes to deciphering lost languages, often a cigar is just a cigar.

3. BE OPEN TO INTERPRETATION.

Remember that some symbols may have multiple meanings. Knowing the approximate date that the carving was made, for example, could help you put the symbol in the proper historical context. The swastika has existed for more than 3,000 years and was used by many cultures as a representation of luck and strength; in the 1930s the Nazis came along and turned it into a symbol connoting quite the opposite. So if you see a swastika in your travels, it doesn't necessarily indicate that the Nazis have been there. Unless you're Indiana Jones, of course, in which case the Nazis are always there. And they're probably coming back. For you.

4. WHEN ALL ELSE FAILS . . . ASK.

Indiana had the headpiece to the Staff of Ra but couldn't make sense of the markings on both sides. Sallah directed him to a local man who could. This is yet another example of the importance of developing embedded contacts in many outposts (see p. 72-77). In this case, the sage old man informed Indy that to determine the proper height of the staff, he had to read both sides of the medallion, something that can't be gathered if the markings on only one side are merely burnt into the palm of a hand. Always look at every item from all sides and all perspectives; otherwise, you run the risk of putting all your kadams in one staff.

5. SAVE IT FOR LATER.

If you're stumped and have no idea what you're looking at and no one to ask for help, you can copy the text, make a rubbing, or take the item in question with you—as long as you are complying with the International Treaty for the Protection of Antiquities, of course.

HOW TO ESCAPE IF YOU ARE
ACCIDENTALLY ENTOMBED

Throughout your career, if you seek to gain the same fortune and glory that Indiana Jones did, you're going to make some enemies along the way. Probably a lot of them. Archaeology is a very competitive field, and, as Dr. Henry Jones Sr. mentioned to his son Indiana while pursuing the Germans to the Canyon of the Crescent Moon, "There's no prize for second place." So true. Many of the artifacts you will seek are unique, priceless treasures. There's only one Holy Grail.

In your attempts to secure these objects, you may find yourself taking extreme risks, and, when that happens, you may have to face the consequences. Indy and Marion Ravenwood learned that the consequences of crossing a mercenary, egocentric archaeologist like Rene Belloq (and his Nazi compadres) was entombment in the Well of Souls, with no one to keep them company but a few thousand asps and some cobras. All in all, a very bad day at the office.

In addition to knowing how to handle himself around snakes (see "The Animal Kingdom," page 98), Jones also had to rely on an astute assessment of his situation and quick and creative problem solving. That was all that kept him and Marion from eventually becoming archaeological finds themselves. Should you end up locked away in a tomb—either by unfortunate accident or at the hands of a megalomaniac—keep the following advice in mind.

WHEN EXPLORING ANCIENT TOMBS, IT'S ALWAYS WISE TO HAVE AN EXIT STRATEGY.

ESCAPE IS EASY...IF YOU HAVE A MULTI-TON STATUE HANDY.

1. BRING BACKUP.

Your best bet, of course, is to avoid getting entombed in the first place. If you are visiting a site on the sly, go with more than one other person and designate someone as lookout. Such a group may attract more attention, but it will also increase the chances that at least one of your partners will be able to go for help. And set off at night. Indy had the sense to do this, although it didn't prevent him from being discovered. Maintain a low profile and camouflage your activities.

2. STAY CALM (SERIOUSLY).

This tip may sound obvious, impossible, or both, but keep in mind what effect jumpiness in a roomful of venomous creatures might have on your chances of a successful escape. Control your breathing. Doing so not only calms you but also uses less oxygen than hyperventilating. You can't change your situation. Your only chance of getting out on your own—as opposed to being dug up by some other archaeologist years later—depends on your ability to focus.

3. LOOK FOR SIGNS OF NATURE.

Take a cue from your surroundings. First, look for light or shadows. A ray of sun may be emanating from an unknown antechamber or crevice; it may indicate a wall with a structural deficiency that you can take advantage of. The same rule applies to evidence of airflow. Stand very still. Do you feel a breeze? Look at any cloth or vine in the room. Is it moving? Figure out what direction the airflow is coming from and start looking there for potential escape routes.

4. LISTEN UP.

Listen for sounds coming from outside the room. Although such noises might not represent a direct exit, they may indicate the presence of another space in the structure. If you can hear through the wall, it may be an indication that the wall has a structural weakness you can exploit.

5. PAY CLOSE ATTENTION TO ANYTHING BREATHING.

Indy wasn't happy about being entombed with thousands of snakes, but part of him was probably relieved. Surely he knew that snakes—especially Egyptian cobras—prefer rodents, fish, birds, and reptiles to insects. So they had to be getting their food from somewhere, which meant they were getting in and out of the chamber somehow. Indy was lucky that their entry point was obvious. The critters were pouring in through holes in the wall.

6. USE YOUR SURROUNDINGS.

As much as it may bother you, some ancient artifacts may have to be sacrificed in order to secure your escape. In Indy's case, giant statues of jackals provided exactly the kind of heft needed to break through the weaker interior wall of the Well of Souls, which the snakes had been using as a turnstile.

HOW TO COPY ANCIENT WRITINGS

Istory is heavy—and we're not talking metaphorically. The ancients wrote their words on all types of materials—parchment, papyrus, wood—but stone is most likely to have survived to the present day. The study of writing etched, chiseled, and scratched into stone, called *epigraphy*, is at the heart of archaeology. When you come upon these writings, they may be inscribed upon something immovable, such as the wall of a cave, a thick stone slab, or a monstrous statue dozens of feet tall. It's simply not feasible to take something that large back to the lab for analysis using X-ray fluorescence. But you still need to harvest that data. What do you do? Thankfully, we have many more options available than Indiana Jones had in his day. But we think you'll agree the method Indy employed is still remarkably viable in the digital age. When you come upon an ancient stone text in the field, here's what to do.

1. ASSESS THE IMPORTANCE OF THE TEXT.

Face it: Even an ancient Egyptian laundry list would be fascinating to modern scientists. The most insignificant writing ought to be interpreted and compared to other existing examples of the same type. But you don't want to waste your time analyzing a piece of text that has already been carefully studied by another scholar—unless you have reason to believe that the other fellow botched the job. Before proceeding with your data collection, get a sense of what you have and if it has ever been analyzed. Chances are, if you're literally treading on new ground, it hasn't.

2. GET SOME LIGHT IN THERE.

Obviously the easiest thing to do is to take a photo of the object. Before you can do so, however, you have to make sure you have enough light to take a decent picture. This won't be easy if you're in tight quarters, many feet below the surface of the earth, or deep inside an ancient temple. If you've traveled with lighting equipment, go to town. But, most likely, you will be simply telling your colleagues to stay the heck out of the light.

3. TAKE DIGITAL AND INSTANT SNAPSHOTS.

Yes, of course you should shoot the object with your digital camera. But you should also snap a few shots with a Polaroid, which will give you an instant hard copy image that won't be lost if the brains of your camera get fried in the hot sun.

4. BACK UP EVERYTHING IMMEDIATELY.

Download the images from your camera to your portable hard drive, and have someone else on your team carry it. If your expedition has access to a satellite link, by all means e-mail the images to your desk at home. This might seem like overkill, but pros like you lose images all the time to luggage theft, sandstorms, technical ignorance, and the occasional plundering nomad. If you traveled this far to get the goods, why take the chance that you'll lose your data? The time to do your backups and uploads is when you're still standing in front of the artifact. After the camels start moving to the next site, you can't go back.

5. WRITE IT DOWN.

Here's where we can all take a tip from Henry Jones Sr. Digital tools sometimes make us so cocky that we don't do the obvious. If something strikes you as important, for gosh sakes, write it down in a notebook and use pencil or waterproof ink, which will stay legible if your book takes a dive in an Italian sewer. Don't forget to sketch any important artwork, too. If the inscription is too large to be transcribed directly, capture the highlights—if you can trust yourself to know what they are—or do a hard-copy capture, as described next in step 6.

6. MAKE A RUBBING.

In 1938, workers employed by the wealthy American businessman Walter Donavan uncovered the first Holy Grail marker in Ankara, Turkey, during a copper excavation. Half of that tablet was missing, so no one could figure out where to begin searching for the Grail. Indiana Jones made a copy of that marker using the only reasonable technology he had: a sheet of tracing paper and a piece of chalk. Later, when he discovered a duplicate marker in a tomb in Venice, he was able to overlay the original tracing onto the second and easily copy the missing half of the inscription. Rubbings have several advantages over photographs: They don't need complex technical equipment, they can sometimes reveal writing that has worn away, and they are infinitely more portable than stone tablets or a camera bag. To make your own, follow these instructions:

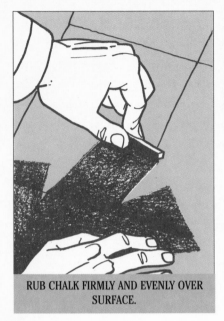

RUB CHALK FIRMLY AND EVENLY OVER
SURFACE.

INSPECT RESULTS FOR ACCURACY.

1. Lay a large sheet of tracing paper over the object to be copied.
   Ask a colleague to hold the paper steady so it won't move. If
   you don't have a beautiful blonde undercover Nazi scientist
   handy, use easy-release tape or artist's gum adhesive. (Be sure
   these materials won't damage the stone surface.)

2. Hold a long piece of dark-colored chalk horizontally and rub
   it firmly down the entire length of the paper. Make sure you
   capture all the writing on the stone. It's smart to check the
   back of the tablet for further inscriptions. (Would anyone ever
   make this mistake after what happened with the headpiece of
   the Staff of Ra?) If you do make a second rubbing, try to do
   it on a second sheet of paper so you can study the pieces side
   by side later.

3. If you expect to be swimming in a sewer later that day, it might be wise to use something other than chalk to make your rubbing. The classic artist's tool, the Conté crayon—manufactured in Paris and invented by Nicolas-Jacques Conté during the Napoleonic wars—is made of compressed clay. It tends to be more durable than ordinary chalk, artist's pastels, or charcoal. But in a pinch, even a crayon will do.

CHAPTER 6

SUPERNATURAL SKILLS

The history of humankind is filled with strange stuff, and archaeologists are often called on to sift through the wreckage. Unfortunately, they're usually on their own when they encounter the bizarre. Zombies, voodoo dolls, the Wrath of God, otherworldly artifacts, bizarre settings, and unnatural beings—Indiana Jones has tangled with them all. To make it back home to his next lecture, he has perfected his skills for coping on the fly. What follows are success strategies to employ when your world goes from fairly typical to paranormal.

HOW TO BREAK A ZOMBIE CURSE

S trictly speaking, zombieism is associated only with the voodoo practitioners of Haiti. A priest or *bokor* places an unsuspecting person under a spell that resembles a near-dead or dead state and thus controls the person's actions. According to legend, zombification was a punishment inflicted upon annoying family members by exasperated kin. One paid a voodoo master to "kill" one's relative, the body was buried, and the victim would later be resuscitated by the priest to live out his natural life as a kind of soulless slave. The veracity of this information is unknown because of the dangers associated with getting close enough to such practitioners to make a thorough, scientific study of the phenomenon. If true, the secrets of zombification are undoubtedly known to shaman-like individuals well beyond Haiti. For example, while recovering the Sankara Stones in India, Indiana Jones was forced to drink a substance described as the blood of the Kali, and he fell into the Black Sleep of the Kali-Ma. In a zombie-like state, he did Mola Ram's bidding without any resistance until he was snapped out of his blood-induced stupor by his ace sidekick, Short Round.

Ethnobotanists theorize that zombie curses have a pharmacological origin. The suspected toxin is tetrodotoxin, the active ingredient found in pufferfish. In large doses, it can kill; in measured doses it slows down one's pulse so much that the victim seems dead. Another substance is later administered to reduce the victim's willpower and bind her to the *bokor* eternally. Since so little is known about these "curses," it's hard to advise what one should do to help a zombified colleague in the field. And since it's entirely possible that the phenomenon is psychosomatic, it is logical to start with the least medically invasive procedure.

1. ASSESS ZOMBIFICATION.

Is the person wandering around subterranean caverns at night? Is he or she displaying a blank, unengaged stare? Does the person pose a threat to himself and others? Is he about to assist in a ritualized human sacrifice? If so, you may have a zombie on your hands.

2. DO THE PERSONAL-RESPONSE TEST.

See if you can establish a personal connection with your zombie friend. Slap his face to see if he "snaps" out of it. Issue commands to see if he will do your bidding. Ask him to explain what has happened to him. If you get no coherent responses, it's time for stronger measures.

3. RESTRAIN AND TRANSPORT THE ZOMBIE TO A SECURE LOCATION.

You've got to get your pal away from the person who has enslaved him. Knock him to the ground, bind or handcuff him, and move him to a safe location, such as your base camp. Watch out: Some zombies are reputed to have the strength of ten men. Get yourself some help and remember to stay on guard until your friend has been awakened from the curse. Otherwise you may find yourself on the evening's sacrificial agenda and inside a giant, human-sized grill.

4. EMPLOY A SHOCK TO THE SYSTEM.

Based on the fact that Indy was awakened from the Black Sleep by the heat of a torch, it seems logical to assume that any powerful physical stimuli might throw the zombified person's body into overdrive, causing them to produce enough adrenalin to override the zombifying agent. While the zombie is still restrained, shock or stun him with whatever you have handy. Don't be shy. Dash him with a bucket of cold water. Swipe his skin with a flaming torch. Pinch or prick his skin with field tools. Rake the surface of his bare skin with the frayed ends of a live lamp cord. Then wait for a response.

5. SEEK MEDICAL TRANSPORTATION.

If nothing's working, use your cell phone or whatever communication means are at your disposal to arrange for medical evacuation. Be sure to bring along all medications the person may have been taking, as well as any evidence that may shed light on your colleague's condition. If, for example, she has recently drunk blood out of a modified skull/funnel apparatus, you might want to pack that skull. Use your gloves.

6. ADMINISTER MEDICATION.

If transportation is slow or nonexistent, administer an epinephrine shot to the heart. Ideally, you will have practiced this technique in a first-aid training course before leaving for your adventure. If not, follow instructions on the syringe packaging. Bear in mind that if you do this poorly, your friend will quickly transition from merely undead to all dead.

NEVER DRINK ANY LIQUID THAT IS SERVED IN A SKULL.

EXTRATERRESTRIALS

The number of academics who believe in the existence of extraterrestrials is surprisingly large, despite that the evidence for such beings is equivocal. Mathematically speaking, life on planets beyond ours is not impossible. What is hard to rationalize—or justify mathematically—is that such life is (a) intelligent, (b) living at a time concurrent to our own, and (c) capable of constructing spacecraft capable of traveling from distant galaxies to Earth. Yet for all these uncertainties, scientists would not be scientists if they did not ask the question, What if? Certainly, it is worth keeping an open mind about the possibility of other dimensions when working in the field. Indeed, many cultures, including our own, embrace and promulgate fascinating bits of folklore surrounding the explanation of unusual phenomena that should definitely be investigated by willing researchers. But if you are ever confronted with beings from other dimensions, it may be smart to do as Indy did and get the heck out of there. As fascinating as aliens may be, you don't want to end up an artifact in another species' museum.

HOW TO DEAL WITH VOODOO DOLLS

The voodoo doll is another relic of the voodoo practice that has jumped the shores of Haiti and landed in black-magic cults of other lands. That should not be much of a surprise, since human beings have always imbued effigies and idols with larger-than-life, supernatural powers. The voodoo doll, however, may be the most personal of the magical totems. The doll is crudely constructed of local materials—straw, burlap, or animal hides—and decorated to resemble the garb and visage of the intended victim. Following incantations, the voodoo master proceeds to "harm" the doll using needles, fire, water, spells, and other methods. The doll's living counterpart reacts as though he or she had been physically harmed. A thrust of a needle feels like the stab of a dagger or lance. The pass of a flame feels like fiery immolation. When the doll is dunked in water, the victim reacts as though he or she is drowning.

Modern science cannot shed much light on this phenomenon. Indeed, the only rational explanation is that the cycle of pain and punishment is accomplished through psychological means, aided by hallucinogens. It's possible that the voodoo master chooses victims that are highly suggestible, shows them the doll, and proceeds with incantations that culminate in the desired result. In a certain emotional state, even the most logical person may respond as though the doll is controlling her actions. Even you, a budding archaeologist, may not be immune to these effects. During his foray among the Thuggees, Indiana Jones was not only coerced into the Black Sleep of the Kali-Ma, but he was also tortured with a voodoo doll that had been shabbily dressed in his trademark leather jacket and fedora. Simply put, if Indy can be voodooed after decades in the field, so can you or your colleague. Here's what to do.

1. MASK YOUR EMOTIONS.

If you've been captured by a gang of raving madmen who appear to be preparing a voodoo doll in your image, try to remain calm. Whatever they say to you, whatever they show you, whatever they do—squelch the impulse to feel and hang onto your power to think. The cognitive state is impartial, rational, and dispassionate. Emotions will weaken your resolve. It helps to remember that you are a man of science and that you are merely observing some strange tribal customs. Take mental notes as though you were gathering information for an ethnography or dissertation.

2. BE UNCOOPERATIVE.

Sure, you may be bound, gagged, and manhandled by beefy men, but you don't have to take it. If captured, you can pretend that you don't understand the language or that you don't hear well. Practice passive resistance; let your body go limp when anyone attempts to make you walk. This makes you much, much heavier to transport. Resist all requests that you partake of any food, drink, or, say, black oily blood.

3. USE ANTI-HYPNOTIC DEFENSES.

Avoid falling into a position where your attention is wholly directed and fixed on a single object or person. Remember, although they may be able to control your surroundings and your body, they cannot control what is going on in your mind if you stand guard at its entrance. If someone appears to be trying to hypnotize you, substitute a competing thought in your mind for everything they say. If they're saying things such as "Maaro maaro sooar ko, chamdi nocho pee lo khoon," think "I need to catalog some artifacts as soon as I get back home."

4. ESCAPE.

The longer their abuse continues, the greater the chance that you may fall into a suggestive state and see the doll as the personification of yourself. Whenever they leave you alone, try to escape. If you're bound, practice rope-evasion techniques (see "How to Break Free If You Are Tied Up," page 93). If you are shackled, use chicanery to extract the key from an inattentive guard. Hang onto your bullwhip; you'll need it to get across moats and crevasses or past obstreperous guards.

5. NAB AND SAFEGUARD THE DOLL.

There's no way to know just how good their magic is. The only way to ensure that you will not be long-distance tortured is to steal the voodoo doll. Resist the temptation to destroy it. It may prove to be a valuable artifact that can finally shed light on this whole voodoo-doll thing. Simply pack it carefully in a sack with sand or rice grains to cushion it for the journey home, and get it back to the lab for analysis. Pack the needles separately.

HOW TO SURVIVE A NUCLEAR BLAST

A nuclear explosion is a scientific phenomenon that is truly akin to a supernatural experience. If you are an archaeologist planning a life in the field, you probably have not considered the possibility of being caught within the vicinity of a nuclear detonation. However, the adventurous life you are choosing means considering every possibility—from enormous insects to supernatural blasts. When you are fending for yourself in the far corners of the world, you must be prepared for everything, and then some. The Wrath of God might be the least of your problems if you find yourself on the wrong side of a nuclear bomb. And while there may be little to nothing you can do about the impending boom, there are a few steps you can take to increase your chances of survival. If you have no way of stopping the blast, keep the following in mind as you prepare for detonation:

1. STAY CALM.

Really. Your wits are your best safeguard under extreme conditions. Keep your fear in check. You can have a breakdown and a cocktail when the dust clears and you are far, far away.

2. ASSESS THE SITUATION.

If you are lucky enough to know how much time remains before the blast, you can better judge your options for escape and shelter. Do some quick mental math, weigh your options, and then . . .

3. MOVE QUICKLY.

Get as far away as you can from the impending blast and put as many potential deterrents as possible between you and the epicenter of the explosion. If there is a vehicle that will speed your journey, take it, whether or not it belongs to you.

4. DO NOT KEEP THE WIND AT YOUR BACK.

As you kick it into high gear away from the blast site—before or after detonation—be sure to travel crosswind (if you have a choice). In other words, do not go directly into or away from the wind, unless, of course, the only available shelter lies in that direction. The wind is the force of nature that will bring the aftermath of doom to your door.

5. GET INDOORS.

Most substances will block at least some radioactivity, but if you can put a substantial barrier between you and the blast, you'll be in better shape. Lead is the top choice, but you're unlikely to find it. Steel and concrete are better alternatives than wood. If you are lucky enough to be within striking distance of a refrigerator, cast-iron bathtub, or, if the gods are really smiling on you, a walk-in meat locker, get inside. This is the one instance when climbing inside a refrigerator is actually a great thing to do. Also, if possible, go deep—underground, that is. Any space underneath a building with a concrete foundation and no windows is a safer spot.

6. MOVE ON.

After the detonation blast, get away before the fallout starts to travel. Fallout shelters are fine as long as someone knows you're in there and can come retrieve you with the proper protective gear. Otherwise, you can't really leave. If you're far enough away from the blast and have managed to shield yourself from the initial blow, get out of there and get as far away as quickly as possible.

7. GET TREATMENT.

If you have been exposed to radiation, you should seek immediate medical attention. Depending on the level, duration, and type of exposure, the results of radiation exposure can range from nothing at all to death. You must get rid of all potentially exposed items—from your skivvies to your cell phone—and take a high-pressure decontamination shower. If you don't think you were exposed, but later experience symptoms of nausea, vomiting, hair loss, nose bleeds, or skin burns, get treatment immediately. It's best to err on the side of caution. And although exposure cannot be reversed, there are a variety of drugs that can help remove the substances from your body.

HOW TO ESCAPE THE WRATH OF GOD

S ometimes archaeologists just can't help themselves. They stick their noses where they don't belong, tamper with artifacts they don't understand, and, in the process, they may unearth powers that have remained hidden for thousands of years.

Just ask the Philistines, who originally snatched the Ark of the Covenant from the Hebrews. Wherever the Philistines took the Ark, some sort of plague or destruction followed. When the death and disease became too much, the Philistines returned the stolen property. Under King Solomon, the Hebrews placed the Ark in a temple. But after Solomon's reign, an Egyptian pharaoh named Shishak came along and—apparently paying no attention to what had happened to the Philistines—took the Ark to Tanis in the Nile Delta. It should be no big surprise that the entire city of Tanis—including the Well of Souls containing the Ark—was soon after buried by a year-long sandstorm. Do you see a pattern here?

There may be some information that we know about religious artifacts, based on folklore, ancient writings, and oral histories. But there is a lot more about these phenomena that we do not know. All we can do is create guidelines based on limited experience. The only time, on record—and those records are hermetically sealed—that the Ark of the Covenant has been opened since it was buried away was in 1936. There were only two (surviving) witnesses to the event—Indiana Jones and Marion Ravenwood—and they both had their eyes closed the entire time. However, they did their best to provide a detailed account based on their

WHEN CONFRONTED WITH THE WRATH OF GOD, CLOSE YOUR EYES.

other four senses. Keep in mind that the suggestions below are based on their experience. They provide no absolute protection from the Wrath of God. No one is that good—not even Indy.

---

1. MINIMIZE THE RISK TO HUMAN LIFE.

Choosing an uninhabited island in the Mediterranean as the site for the ceremonial opening of the Ark was one of the better choices made by Rene Belloq, Colonel Dietrich, and Gestapo agent Arnold Toht. Should the Ark again be opened, it would be a wise choice to do the same and thus limit the loss of innocent life.

---

2. DRESS FOR THE OCCASION.

Donning your best ceremonial gear to crack open a relic shrouded in mystery and foreboding religious lore may add an air of authenticity to the occasion, and perhaps God will appreciate your formality. But it takes much more than some fancy clothes to pull one over on the Wrath. Wearing a headpiece and carrying a staff doesn't make you any match for the fire-breathing minions of the afterlife.

---

3. PUT AWAY THE CAMERA.

You will, of course, be tempted to commit the historical event to your permanent film archives, but this will prove harder than you think. You should know that all electrical devices you have so painstakingly brought to the site will be completely disabled. Unleashing the Wrath of God is akin to setting off an ancient electromagnetic pulse bomb—the E-M-P of G-O-D.

Filming, in general, is not a good idea. Do you think these artifacts were hidden away in the sand for 3,000 years because the powers-that-be wanted them to be shown and re-shown on YouTube?

4. DON'T BE FOOLED BY GOOD LOOKS.

Part of the allure of otherworldly powers is that they are enticing and beautiful, and, at the same time, extremely forceful and deadly. Like the Sirens seductively beckoning sailors to their deaths, dates from hell will swoop around you, rendering you delirious in their magnificent pulchritude. But beauty can be deceiving, and these ethereal creatures will soon morph into hold-on-to-your-lunch terrors. Don't ever forget that they are messengers from the beyond who have been locked away for a very, very long time. And they are mad.

5. DON'T LOOK.

If you truly want to escape the Wrath of God, here is the best piece of advice we can offer. Don't look at it. Really. The only thing we know for sure is that Jones and Ravenwood survived, and they both kept their eyes closed. There are just some things we are not meant to see. So, if you'd like to avoid the fiery consumption, melting your torso and face like one of Madame Tussaud's creations in a heat wave, exploding your head, and dissolving as every vestige of your corporeal being is sucked into the heavens, then keep your eyes closed and mind your own business.

NORTH AMERICA
Washington D.C.
Boston
Charleston
Bahama Islands
San Francisco
California
Gulf of Mexico
MEXICO
CARIBBEA
Guatumala
Galapagos Islands
130
140
EQUATOR
Iles Marquises
SOUTH PACIFIC
TROPIC OF CANCER
Easter Island